THE
ROAD
TO
MERCY

D0910627

THE
ROAD
TO
MERCY

A JOURNEY OF SECRETS, SURVIVAL, AND REDEMPTION

MARY THERESE HUTCHINSON

ISBN 978-1-7342295-0-9 (print)
ISBN 978-1-7342295-1-6 (ebook)

Contact author at **www.marytheresehutchinson.com**

Book and E-Book designed and formatted by
www.ebooklistingservices.com

Cover design by Valentina Brunetto (Vahliable) at
www.99designs.com

Author photo by Gregory Chouffi

Publisher's Cataloging-in-Publication Data
Names: Hutchinson, Mary Therese, author.
Title: The road to mercy: a journey of secrets, survival, and redemption / Mary Therese Hutchinson.
Description: Richmond, VA: Power Filled Press, 2019.
Identifiers: LCCN: 2019917780 | ISBN: 978-1-7342295-0-9 (pbk.) | 978-1-7342295-1-6 (ebook)
Subjects: LCSH Hutchinson, Mary Therese. | Christian biography--United States. | Adult child abuse victims--United States--Biography. | Abused children--United States--Biography. | Sexual abuse victims--Biography. | Self-actualization (Psychology) | BISAC BIOGRAPHY & AUTOBIOGRAPHY / Personal Memoirs.
Classification: LCC HV6626.52 .H88 2019 | DDC 362.76/092--dc23

1 3 5 7 9 10 8 6 4 2
Printed in the United States of America

DEDICATION

To my courageous husband Wally, who has encouraged, supported, and aided me in bringing this book to fruition, warts and all.

To my brave Mom, who struggled through life on her own for many years. You're not alone anymore.

To my angelic brother Ed, a role model for us all. The world would be a much better place if there were more people like you.

TABLE OF CONTENTS

ACKNOWLEDGEMENTS

Any credit for this book belongs to God, as it was his idea for me to tell the story of what he did in my life. Words cannot express my gratitude for all he has done.

I am also grateful to two people who were instrumental in my becoming a Christian. Arthur was obedient to God when asked to pray for me even though he didn't know me. Jean led me to Christ when she was a new Christian herself.

I would like to thank my editor Jeanette Windle for the tremendous amount of work she spent on bringing this manuscript to a professional level. Also Amy Deardon of www.ebooklistingservices.com for handling all the technical and graphic design aspects of the print and eBook publication.

I would like to thank my husband Wally and my twin Chrissy for their input and encouragement as well as my friends for their prayers and support in making this book a reality. Also my team of proofreaders who were invaluable in this project.

A special thanks to Investigator Williams who went above and beyond as he located the crime scenes.

I also wish to thank Kerry Livgren, member of the rock group Kansas, who gave me permission to use the lyrics to his hit song, "Dust in the Wind."

PROLOGUE

And I will restore to you the years that the locust hath
eaten.

—Joel 2:25(a)

G od spared me from being murdered. Not once. Not twice.
But four times. In one night. I was twelve years old.

As a young girl attending a Catholic school in Upstate New
York in the mid-1950s, I was taught about God. I believed he was
real. I wanted him to be real. But then bad things happened to me.
Again. And again.

Because of those traumatic events, I came to believe that
everything I was taught about God must have been a fairy tale.
After all, if he was real, how could he allow such horrible things to
happen to me? To top it off, I was threatened to keep most of what
I endured a secret.

As a young adult, I was consumed with a "why me" attitude
that included anger and shame among other negative emotions. I

had no hope of feeling normal or being in a healthy relationship. Those were things I could possess only in my dreams.

I was twenty-four years old when God asked a stranger to pray for me. Though I knew nothing about this at the time, it was the beginning of a turnaround in my life. Instead of continuing down a dark, twisting road to despair and self-destruction, I found myself on a road to mercy. A mercy I did not in any way deserve from a heavenly Father whose boundless, unconditional love for me I could never have envisioned.

My spiritual journey along that road has been a long one with its own twists and turns more dramatic at times than any fictional tale. But in the end it has led to emotional healing and a dramatic transformation. And eventually God did make all my dreams come true even more than I could have imagined.

I know now that God is not a fairy tale. He is very real, and he changes lives. He certainly changed mine. I don't know why he spared my life, but I owe it to him to tell what happened. I also owe it to everyone else who has yet to discover the reality of God's existence, the boundless extent of God's love and mercy, and the relationship he desires to have with them.

What God did for me, he can do for you as well and for anyone who seeks the freedom only he can give. My prayer in sharing my story in these pages is that you will find the same road to mercy I have found. And that you will follow that road straight into the embrace of a loving heavenly Father who yearns to give you too a second chance.

CHAPTER ONE

Sealed Lips

The sorrows of death compassed me.

—Psalm 18:4(a)

I promise I won't tell," I told Uncle Norman.

As soon as I said those words, my uncle pulled his vehicle out of the fast-food drive-in's parking lot and back onto the road. Tension and cigarette smoke permeated the car's interior, and I shrank away from him as far as I could in the front passenger seat. I didn't own a watch, but it felt well past midnight, and the only lights I could see on that darkened country highway shone from the headlights of my uncle's ten-year-old 1957 Pontiac and an occasional passing vehicle.

I know Mom must be worried about me by now!

We had left my home in Upstate New York hours earlier when Uncle Norman offered to take me to the store. I'd wanted to buy Mom a Valentine's card to give her the next day with a heart-shaped box of chocolates I'd hidden in my dresser drawer. It wasn't unusual for me to be out with Uncle Norman, who'd moved into our home a year earlier after my father—his brother—disappeared from our lives. But it was the first time we were out so late on a school night.

It wasn't long before a one-story brick state police station appeared ahead of us. As my uncle pulled his Pontiac into the well-lit parking lot, I stared out the front window, petrified he would change his mind about turning himself in.

Exhaling a puff of smoke, Uncle Norman turned towards me. "Remember what you're supposed to say."

"I remember." I wasn't about to forget those orders.

I took a deep breath as we entered the small station, too terrified to appreciate the safety of my new surroundings. The police would soon question me about what had happened, and I was afraid they wouldn't believe our fictitious story. The weight on my twelve-year-old shoulders felt overwhelming, and I just wanted the nightmare to go away.

I don't know what all my uncle said to the police officer at the front desk, but before I even had to give any account of what had happened, an officer was asking for my home phone number to call my mom. Then another whisked me away to the nearest hospital. The officer waited in the reception area while an emergency room nurse took me into a curtained section where I changed into a hospital gown.

A doctor came in moments later. As he looked me over, he made a comment to the nurse about the massive amount of blood in my hair. He then removed a bandage over my left eye, observing that the laceration above my eye couldn't be the source of all the blood. The nurse seemed to be taking notes of what he said.

"Were you hit with anything?" he asked me.

"Just my uncle's fists and hands," I answered simply.

Separating strands of my blood-soaked hair with a puzzled expression, the doctor soon discovered the laceration on top of my head. "Are you sure you weren't hit with a bottle?"

"I didn't see a bottle," I responded cautiously. *I can't tell him the truth, no matter what!*

The doctor discovered a third laceration hidden underneath my hair above my left ear. "You're going to need a few stitches, young lady. But we'll have to shave away some of your hair first."

"Oh, no!" I could no longer hold back my tears. My hair was a big deal to me, and I didn't want to lose any of it.

"We just need to shave a little around each of the wounds. It won't even be noticeable," the doctor consoled me. "But first I need to numb those wounds."

"With a needle?"

"Yes. One in each wound. It will only hurt for a second."

I caught a glimpse of the enormous needle as the doctor held it behind his back. He tried to distract me with conversation, but it was too late for that.

"Ouch!" Closing my eyes, I let out a yell at each painful needle stab. Tears streamed down my battered face. I was so relieved when he finished.

After he stitched up my wounds, the doctor examined the rest of my body. The nurse continued to make notes as he reported on the contusions around my eyes, nose, and neck, the scratches on my throat, and my swollen nose. He paused his report to ask me, "Did you get hit in the nose?"

"No, it's always been this big." I'd hated my nose for years and always considered it to be too big. I didn't realize that my nose was actually swollen because it had just been broken. For some reason, the doctor never x-rayed or treated it.

The doctor examined my swollen and bruised right ring finger, determined it was sprained, and put a splint on it. Then he told me he needed to examine my private parts. I was humiliated and couldn't wait for the exam to be over. By the time he finished, Mom had arrived, our next-door neighbor Phyllis right behind her. I could see that Mom was still wearing her flannel pajamas underneath her winter coat.

"My baby! My poor baby! Are you okay?" Mom screamed hysterically as she hugged me. "How could he do this to my baby?"

She finally calmed down enough to ask what had happened. Staying on script, I told her that Uncle Norman had pulled his car over and started beating on me.

"Why would he do that?" she asked.

"I don't know." I hated lying to Mom, but I felt it was my only option. I could tell she was in disbelief, trying to process what had occurred, as was I.

"I did an internal exam, and it appears your daughter wasn't raped," the doctor said.

"You did what?" Mom yelled. "Who gave you permission to look at her private parts?"

Uh, oh! The doctor was in trouble now! He quickly explained to my mom why he'd examined me. She eventually calmed down but still insisted the examination was totally unnecessary. To Mom, the possibility that Uncle Norman might have sexually assaulted me was inconceivable.

Once I was released from the hospital, the officer informed my mom that he was taking us back to the police station so I could give my statement to the investigator. Our neighbor Phyllis could follow in her own car. It was still dark by the time we left the hospital. As we got into the trooper's car, Mom asked me again about what had happened. I gave the same short explanation about Uncle Norman beating me.

"I don't understand why he would do such a thing," she said.

That makes two of us!

Mom talked non-stop to the officer about Uncle Norman all the way to the station. "I can't understand why my brother-in-law would harm my daughter. I've known him for over fifteen years. He's been like a brother to me. He's never shown any sign of violent behavior. I've never even had an argument with him. This is completely out of character for the man I've known all these years. I just don't understand why he would do this!"

In between talking to the officer, she would turn her attention back to me, hugging me, patting me, asking over and over if I was okay. I just shrugged numbly, not wanting to have to tell my false story again.

Pulling back into the police station parking lot, the officer walked me inside with Mom and Phyllis following behind. I'd been relieved to be able to stick with Uncle Norman's version of our story at the hospital and to Mom. Now I'd have to put on an Oscar-worthy performance for the police.

Behind me, I suddenly heard Mom scream. "Where is he? I'll kill him!"

Thankfully, Uncle Norman was nowhere in sight or who knows what Mom might have done to him. The officer calmed her down, then introduced us to Investigator Bianco, who'd been assigned to the case.

"I'm going to need to get a statement from both of you," Investigator Bianco told us. He led Mom into his office to take her statement first.

Phyllis and I waited in the main area where there were desks and workstations for the officers. Through a large glass window, I could see Mom sitting at a chair in front of the investigator's desk. The investigator sat across from her, a typewriter in front of him, on which he occasionally typed as my mom's mouth moved.

I wonder what he's asking her! Next to me, Phyllis was talking, but I wasn't paying attention, my eyes glued on Mom and the investigator. Over and over, I rehearsed in my mind what Uncle Norman had told me to say. Then I saw Mom and the investigator stand up and knew it was my turn. Suddenly I felt nauseous.

Emerging into the main room, Mom came over to where Phyllis and I were sitting. She gestured to Investigator Bianco, who had followed her out. "Just tell him what Uncle Norman did."

That's not going to happen! I followed the investigator into his office. The small room was cramped, its walls lined with file cabinets. Seating me in the room's only chair where my mom had been sitting, he sat behind his desk and slid a fresh piece of paper into his typewriter. "I'm going to ask you a few questions. Then I'll type out your answers."

"Okay," I nodded. *I need to get this right. If he doesn't believe me, Uncle Norman will find out and kill me for sure this time!*

"What is your name and address?"

Giving him the information, I stared at the investigator's large, muscular hands as he used just his two index fingers to rapidly peck out my answer on the typewriter.

"And how old are you?"

"Twelve."

He raised his eyes to look intently into my face. "Now can you tell me what happened last night on February 13, 1967?"

"Well, I went for a ride with my Uncle Norman, who lives with us." I was glad when the investigator's focus dropped from my face back to his typewriter keys. "He drove outside of town to do some errands. Then he pulled over and started beating me in the face and on my head with his fists."

The investigator continued with his rapid pecking motions. My cracking voice must have told him how nervous I was, but he never mentioned it. He may have simply attributed it to my being a child who had just gone through a traumatic ordeal. What he didn't realize was that my anxiety actually stemmed from fear that he wouldn't believe me.

"Do you know why he hit you?"

"No." *At least that answer is true.*

"Did he hit you with anything?"

Oh no, here we go again with that question!

"I didn't see anything."

"What time was it?"

"I don't know, but it was already dark."

"What happened next?"

"Uncle Norman just drove around until he pulled in next to a telephone booth in a fast-food drive-in parking lot. He told me he was going to call the operator to find the location of the nearest police station. He did that, then drove around looking for this station. He finally found it, and we both came inside."

That was the extent of my statement. Rolling the document out of the typewriter, the investigator asked me to sign it. He then pulled a Polaroid instant camera out of his desk and took a photo of me from the neck up. "Okay, we're finished here."

I was so relieved as we walked back out to where Mom and Phyllis waited. Since the investigator hadn't questioned my answers, I was confident I had indeed put on an award-winning performance fueled by my desire to survive. One of the officers spoke to Mom for a few more minutes. Then he said we could leave.

The sun had just come up as Mom, Phyllis, and I headed towards Phyllis's car, which was parked on the far side of Uncle

Norman's. As I walked past, I could see that the front passenger seat was covered with massive blood stains. My stomach became queasy, and I quickly turned away. Neither Mom nor Phyllis mentioned it, so I assumed they were too distracted to look inside. No one could have imagined what happened in that car. I couldn't even believe it, and I was the one who had lived through it.

Climbing into the back seat of Phyllis's car with me, Mom wrapped me in her arms. The entire hour-long ride, she either sobbed, yelled about Uncle Norman, or thanked God I was alive.

"The officer told me Norman confessed to hitting you," Mom said. "He told the officer that God made him stop. I was praying for you last night when you were gone so long. Now I know God heard my prayers!"

Still imprisoned by fear of the consequences if I told, I couldn't comprehend what she said. As I gazed out the car window, I felt as if a darkness had been following me my entire life. I determined in that moment to never speak the truth about what happened.

No one would pry those secrets out of my mouth.

Not ever.

CHAPTER TWO

Once Upon a Time

Before I formed thee in the belly I knew thee.

—Jeremiah 1:5(a)

My paternal grandfather, Cary Robarde, Sr., known to his relatives as the "black sheep" of the family, consumed massive amounts of beer and stayed intoxicated for six months out of the year. When sober, he worked as a plumber in Upstate New York. My paternal grandmother bore him six children in seven years. Very little is known about my grandmother, whom I never met and who passed away when I was a small child.

Unlike my grandfather, his cousins were upstanding local tradesmen with their own businesses. The Robarde family even had a street named after them.

The eldest sibling, my father Cary Jr., was born just a few years before the start of the worst economic crisis to hit the United States. The Great Depression began after the stock market crashed in October of 1929 and lasted throughout the 1930s.

Unemployment broke all previous records as did homelessness and the need for soup kitchens. My grandfather's drinking left his own family even more poverty-stricken.

My grandparents were Catholic by heritage. Due to the extreme poverty they were experiencing during the Depression, they were forced to place my father and his younger siblings in various Catholic orphanages and foster homes. When my father was twelve, his father took him out of the orphanage to live at home while his siblings remained behind. Most of the time, the cupboards were bare except for bread and mustard. My father dropped out of school before the ninth grade.

When my father was thirteen, he noticed the next-door neighbor, Mrs. Haskell, unloading groceries from her car. He offered to carry them in for a small fee, and she agreed. When he told her he needed the money for food, she hired him to help with her weekly groceries. For the next several years, she and her husband often fed him.

The economy turned around when World War II began. My father turned eighteen in 1942, at which point he joined the army, fighting in the Pacific.

Mom's story mirrors my father's. Marie Bouchand was born in 1928 to Catholic parents in Upstate New York. One of six siblings, she was two years old when the Depression hit. That year, one of the neighbors noticed Mom sitting in the middle of the street as a huge truck headed towards her. Helpless, the neighbor watched in horror and then amazement as the undercarriage drove over Mom. She survived with only a minor head injury.

The Bouchand family was also extremely poor, and when Mom was four, she and her siblings ended up in different foster homes and Catholic orphanages. Mom was placed in St. Cecelia's Catholic Orphanage. It was there she learned about God and Jesus. When she was five, she was placed in a foster home with Herman and Mildred Blackburn. She lived with them for nine years. During part of that time, two of her five siblings were also sent to live there, including Agnes, a year older than Mom, and Frank, a year younger, who had polio.

The Blackburns were Catholic as well and took Mom and her siblings to church on Sundays. Mom had been baptized as an infant and made her First Communion and Confirmation while living with the Blackburns.

But Mildred Blackburn had two personas—the one seen in public with the children on Sundays and a very different one behind closed doors. Her severe dark features resembled those of the Wicked Witch of the West in *The Wizard of Oz*.

Mom was always hungry when she lived with the Blackburns. Sometimes she would take a piece of food without permission. If Mildred discovered it, she would beat Mom on the head with a large brown bowl. She would also force Mom to brush her hair for hours. If Mom stopped, she would get a painful poke in the ribs.

Mom's own mother visited only once while she lived with the Blackburns, and her father never visited. At fourteen, Mom was transferred back to the orphanage. As at the Blackburns, food portions were small at St. Cecelia's, and Mom remained hungry again most of the time. She also had to work long hours in the laundry room. But she was treated kindly by the nuns, and it felt like heaven compared to the Blackburns.

While at St. Cecilia's, Mom attended catechism classes, where she learned the teachings of the Catholic Church. She also had a beautiful singing voice and would sing on stage during holiday performances. This was her greatest pleasure during her time at the orphanage, and she loved every minute of it.

At eighteen, Mom was no longer a ward of the state. She moved into St. Cecilia's Infant Orphanage where a live-in program trained young women to care for infants. Successful students earned a Child Technician Certificate upon completion. Many of the young women at the Infant Orphanage wanted to become nuns once they finished the program. Mom was one of those young women.

Mom had a week before she needed to report to St. Cecelia's for training, so she decided to visit her sister Agnes, whom she hadn't seen in a year. Agnes had her own tiny apartment in a town less than a half hour bus ride from St. Cecilia's, where she worked as a secretary. Packing her one small suitcase with a few belongings, Mom rode the bus to Agnes's neighborhood. When she arrived, she could hear voices coming from inside the apartment before she knocked on the door.

"Who is it?" she heard her sister's voice call out.

"It's Marie. I have a week's vacation, and I thought I would come and stay with you."

"I have company," Agnes responded without opening the door.

"When can I come back?" Mom asked.

"I'm busy," Agnes shouted through the door. "You can't stay here."

"What about tomorrow?" Mom asked, near tears.

"No, not tomorrow either!"

Tears rolling down her cheeks, Mom walked to Woolworth's Department Store, carrying her little suitcase. After hanging out there for a few hours, she headed to a nearby park. For several more hours, she sat on a bench watching squirrels chase each other and pigeons looking for food. She wondered about the lives of the people strolling past. WWII had been over for a year now, and things were getting back to normal.

Night was beginning to fall, and Mom didn't know where she could go. Then she remembered seeing a restroom in the hallway of Agnes's apartment building. Walking back there, she locked herself into the bathroom and slept on the floor. For the rest of the week, she hung out in the park and Woolworth's during the day and slept on the bathroom floor at night until it was time to return to St. Cecelia's.

After my father's release from the army, he kept in touch with his siblings. His youngest sister Irene was nineteen and lived at St. Cecilia's in the same program as Mom. Several years earlier, another sister, Evelyn, had snuck out through the window of her room at St. Cecilia's, heading off to New York City in hopes of becoming a model.

One day my father arrived at St. Cecilia's to take his sister Irene out to eat. While he waited outside for her, he lit up a cigarette. As he did so, he noticed an attractive young woman with Italian features and long, dark wavy hair looking out of an upstairs window.

Emerging outside, Irene asked, "Are you ready to go, Cary?"

"Who is that up there in the window?" he responded, eyes locked on the young woman behind the glass pane.

"That's my new roommate, Marie."

"She's very pretty. I'd like to go out with her."

"You'll never get her to go out with you," Irene chuckled. "She wants to become a nun."

"Just introduce me to her," he ordered his sister. "I'll get her to go out with me."

Cary had a lot of experience in the dating game from his time in the army and since his release, while Marie had none. She resisted his attempts for a while, but his persuasive personality, good looks, and determination eventually wore her down. With his wavy, reddish-blond hair and short stature, he was often told of his striking resemblance to James Cagney, a famous actor from the 1920s to the present day.

One day after several months of dating, Mom told my father she didn't want to see him anymore, insisting she still wanted to become a nun. But when the holiday season arrived, my father grew lonely. Visiting Mom, he convinced her to date him again. Just a few months later, they married at St. Paul's Catholic Church in a private ceremony with Agnes as one of their two witnesses.

Agnes and her boyfriend doubled-dated with my parents from time to time. My father also helped Mom look for the rest of her family. Those they were able to locate weren't interested in having a relationship, and the others were never found.

My father worked making deliveries for a local linen-cleaning company while Mom worked at a factory. They found a cute little bungalow for sale but couldn't afford the down payment, so they borrowed the money from my father's brother Murray, who also worked at a local factory. They bought the house and were very content.

During their second year of marriage, Mom miscarried. Two years later, she conceived again. Mom was eight months pregnant when she went into labor on a drizzly morning in the summer of 1954. Shortly after noon, she gave birth to a little girl. My parents had decided beforehand that if the baby was a girl, they would name her Christine and call her Chrissy.

Moments later the doctor made an announcement. "Mrs. Robarde, you have another baby on the way."

"Twins?" Mom cried out. "But I only have one sweater set."

Ten minutes later, I made my unexpected entrance into this world.

CHAPTER THREE

Pack Your Bags

But my God shall supply all your need.

—Philippians 4:19(a)

T wins?" my father exclaimed with stunned shock when given the news in the hospital waiting room.

My parents were not prepared for twins, so this was quite an adjustment. Because of my low birth weight and other medical problems, I was kept in the hospital for a month while Chrissy went home. Every day Mom would go to the hospital and check up on me.

She also called her sister as soon as she could to let her know of our birth. But Agnes's reaction was not what she'd hoped. "What are you telling me for? Do you want a gift?"

"No, I thought you'd be happy for me," Mom responded.

"Didn't you learn enough from our past?" Agnes yelled. "And now you bring two more babies into this world? Don't call me anymore."

Mom was able to locate her brother Frank as well, whom she hadn't seen in years, to give him the news. But when he came by for a visit, he was intoxicated and vulgar. Mom told him not to come around unless he was sober, and she didn't hear from him again.

Chrissy and I were baptized at St. Paul's Catholic Church where my parents married. Mom gave up her job to care for us.

Later that year my father's employer promised him a promotion with higher pay if he would agree to transfer to Tulsa, Oklahoma, where they had another branch. With two more mouths to feed, my father accepted the job offer. Chrissy and I were just nine months old when my parents sold their little bungalow, repaid the down payment they'd borrowed from Uncle Murray, and headed to Tulsa with hopes for a better future.

But Mom wasn't happy in Tulsa. She had never traveled more than thirty miles from home and didn't want to live so far away where she didn't know anyone. One day when my father's sister Evelyn called, Mom poured out her discontent. "It's so lonely here! And Cary never received the promotion he was promised."

"You need to move to New York City," her sister-in-law suggested. "I have a friend who can get Cary a job."

My father took his sister up on the offer, and we moved for the second time in a year, this time into a tiny apartment my parents rented in a lower income neighborhood of NYC. Evelyn's friend never came through with the promised job, but my father convinced the owner of a diner that he was an experienced cook and was hired on the spot.

Still, supporting us on his meager salary was a struggle for my father, and Mom didn't like the area, feeling it was an unsafe environment to raise children. So after just a few months, my parents moved back to their hometown in Upstate New York. They rented another small apartment, and my father found a job as a local truck driver delivering milk. Discontented, he didn't stay long at that job.

"One of these days we're going to California," he'd say to Mom. "Just wait and see."

He found other jobs but each time left voluntarily or was let go. More often than not, he was unemployed. With my father's job instability, our family's financial situation plummeted even further. He would disappear for days or weeks at a time, sometimes with his youngest brother Ron. Each time he told Mom he was leaving to find work.

More than once during my father's absences, Mom ran out of food and money. She would call the nuns at St. Cecilia's for help, who provided the food we needed to survive. One year just before Thanksgiving, our cupboards were bare and our electricity had been cut off. With her situation so dire, Mom once again mustered up enough courage to call the nuns.

That very day our electricity was turned back on. We also received a delivery of groceries, including a turkey and other necessary ingredients for a full Thanksgiving meal. Mom was cooking the Thanksgiving dinner when my father walked in with his brother Ron. Mom chewed him out for leaving us penniless on Thanksgiving.

My father just shrugged off her criticism. "I wasn't worried. I knew the nuns would provide."

Another time in the summer, my father took off, leaving us with no food in the house. Mom hesitated to tell the nuns my father had left her destitute again. With no one else to ask for help, she decided to take Chrissy and me to a nearby park while she figured out what to do. Sitting on a bench while Chrissy and I played nearby, she broke into sobs.

Just then a short, plump woman waddled towards her. Dressed in a plain house dress with gray hair pinned up in a bun, she was the stereotype of a sweet, elderly grandmother. Peering through black-framed eyeglasses, she asked, "Are you okay?"

"No," Mom responded, tears running down her cheeks. "My husband is off somewhere looking for work, and I have no money to buy food or milk for my twins."

The stranger introduced herself as Hazel. Though of humble means herself, she took Mom to the store and bought her groceries. Mom learned that Hazel and her husband owned a little house nearby. Hazel cleaned houses by day and offices by night, while her husband worked as a school custodian.

Thus began a friendship that lasted until Hazel's death. Over the years Hazel often bought us what little groceries she could. She also provided us with used clothes from her nieces, who were also twins and several years older than Chrissy and me. Many of those outfits were even identical as were often worn by twins.

Though in fact, Chrissy and I looked no more alike than any other two siblings. This was because we were fraternal twins, which means we developed from two different fertilized eggs and had different DNA. In contrast, identical twins develop from one fertilized egg and have the same DNA. My hair was medium-brown, thick, and curly while Chrissy's was dark-brown, thin, and straight. We both had hazel eyes, but hers had more brown than mine.

Still, we looked quite similar during our toddler years and cute enough in our twin outfits that passersby often paused to ooh and aah. Hazel came to love us dearly and grew frustrated with my father's lack of provision for his family. She informed Mom about a public assistance program for poor single parents. She suggested Mom leave my father in order to be eligible for the program, but Mom refused.

Eventually, Uncle Murray pulled some strings to get my father a job at the factory where Uncle Murray had worked for years. Mom was relieved that my father finally had a steady job with a salary sufficient to provide for our family. But just two weeks later, he arrived home early from work.

"Why are you home early?" Mom asked.

"I quit," my father responded.

Mom's voice rose. "You did what?"

"I quit. I'm not going to punch a clock for the rest of my life."

"What are we going to do now?" Mom asked in tears.

"I'll find something else."

But weeks went by without my father finding any work. Mom finally approached him. "The landlord keeps asking when we're going to pay the back rent."

The next morning my father went out, returning later in the day with an announcement. "Pack up. I found another apartment. Ron will be here at midnight to move us out."

"We can't keep sneaking out on the landlord like this."

"We won't," my father shrugged. "One of these days we're going to California."

Once in the new apartment, things went back to normal with my father working at whatever job he could find. Because of our income level and her connection to the nuns, Mom was able to enroll Chrissy and me in kindergarten at St. Mary's Catholic School for free, including our uniforms. It was there I learned about God and Jesus and came to believe they were real. The nuns also taught us the Ten Commandments and formal prayers, such as the Our Father, also known as the Lord's Prayer, and the Hail Mary.

From time to time when there was extra money for supplies, Mom drew beautiful portraits on canvas, many of which were various Catholic saints. I watched in awe as Mom painted them in oils. Some of her paintings were given to St. Cecilia's Orphanage and displayed on their walls.

When Chrissy and I were five, my father ran off with a waitress named Jill from the diner where he was working. That was the catalyst for Mom to finally sign up for public assistance. After only a week, the escapade with Jill ended and my father returned home.

"I called the diner looking for you," Mom said. "I know about Jill."

"I'm sorry," my father said. "It's over now."

"It's too late," Mom told him. "I already signed up for welfare. If I take you back, I won't qualify for their benefits."

My father was confident he could get Mom to change her mind. The following week he came to see us, begging her to take him back. But Mom refused. She told him their children's survival depended on her decision. What neither of them knew was that Mom was pregnant again. When Mom broke the news to my father, he stopped asking to return home.

With the help of a friend, Mom moved us to a three-bedroom apartment in a much smaller nearby town where housing was less expensive. Built in 1890, the four-unit residence had a large fenced-in backyard lined with purple lilac trees. The apartment did have its drawbacks. There were only two gas-burning heaters to keep five rooms warm. The bathroom was cold and had no sink. The kitchen's dingy linoleum floor was slanted, so we had to tuck folded-up newspaper under one leg of our Formica kitchen table to keep it level.

On the plus side, everything we needed—grocery store, laundromat, bakery, bank, department store, post office, and other businesses—was within walking distance. This was a huge help since the family didn't own a car.

The public elementary school was only two blocks away, but Mom insisted on sending us to St. Mark's Catholic School, almost a mile away. Once again, she used her connection with the nuns at St. Cecilia's to enroll Chrissy and me into first grade at St. Mark's. Our tuition, uniforms, shoes, and lunches were free.

My father came to visit as the weeks progressed. He got a job and paid Mom child support. I cried each time he said goodbye. But just a few months after our move, my father moved to Massachusetts to live with his brother Ron, who was now living there.

Chrissy and I had turned six when our younger brother Ed was born. My father visited occasionally after he moved away but eventually stopped. When Mom didn't hear from him for a while, she called Uncle Ron and asked to speak to my father.

"Cary moved out," Uncle Ron told her.

"Where did he go?" Mom asked.

"He didn't say. He just packed up and left about six weeks ago. I haven't heard from him since."

Mom called my father's other siblings, but none of them knew his whereabouts either. He had simply vanished.

Chapter Four

Monkey Meat

It is written, man shall not live by bread alone.

—Matthew 4:4(a)

D ay in and day out, I wondered where my father was and when he was coming back. His decision to abandon us devastated me and caused a deep sense of loss as well as low self-esteem.

Despite the advantages of a big yard, nearby shopping, and plenty of room, we also soon discovered additional drawbacks in our new living situation. Though Mom kept the apartment immaculate, we constantly battled cockroaches in our kitchen. They came out only at night, scattering when someone turned on the kitchen light.

As much as Mom tried, she couldn't get rid of the roaches. She complained to the landlord, but only after repeated requests did he bother to fumigate. To air out the apartment, we had to leave the windows open for days. While it did get rid of the roaches, others returned within a few months. The landlord refused to fumigate again, so we either used roach spray or crushed them on sight. I found them disgusting and hated them with a passion.

Then one day while sitting on the toilet, I spotted a mouse running by. Raising my legs as high as I could, I screamed, "M-o-m-m-y!"

Since the bathroom door was closed, I felt trapped. I must have scared the mouse because when I looked around for it, I saw it shimmying down a hole behind the toilet where a large pipe ran up through the ceiling. When I told Mom what had happened, she put out a mouse trap. We caught that mouse, but others showed up. Mom stuffed the hole with rags, but still they squeezed through. For years whenever I used the toilet, I sat there on alert with feet raised and got out of that room as fast as I could.

The high ceilings made heating the apartment difficult with just two gas heaters, so during the frigid winter months Mom would turn on the stovetop burners and oven for extra heat. The floor next to the large space heater in the living room became the most coveted seat in the apartment. When our couch and chair cushions wore out, there was no money to replace them. Applying her creativity, Mom instead stuffed them with old clothes and purchased slipcovers to cover them.

By now our younger brother Ed was old enough we needed to keep our eyes on him at all times. A little escape artist, he'd figured out how to turn the lock latch underneath the doorknob on the back door. Numerous times he was found by a neighbor running down the street in his underwear. A hook-and-eye latch was installed at the top of the door to keep him from escaping, but Ed was so smart he figured out how to use a broom handle to lift the hook out of the eye. Staying one step ahead of him was a constant chore.

Mom became good friends with our next-door neighbor Phyllis, who was married but had no children. Phyllis owned a car, and once a month she would take either Chrissy or me to the fire station on the other side of town to pick up our monthly allotment of government surplus food. This included peanut butter, cheese, oatmeal, butter, and other staples as well as various kinds of canned meats. We nicknamed one of the canned meats, which looked like processed ham, "monkey meat."

Mom couldn't afford to pay Phyllis for taking us to pick up our food, so she paid her with some of the surplus items. Each month Phyllis would make us delicious oatmeal cakes with some of the supplies Mom gave her. As much as I looked forward to those wonderful cakes, I dreaded the humiliation of standing in line for government handouts. It didn't bother Mom, though. To her they were a much-needed provision for her family as they supplemented the groceries she bought with her welfare money.

My mom actually learned to cook from my father, who had worked as a short order cook, and her creativity showed in the kitchen as well as in her art. When food got scarce at the end of the month, she broke up bread into a bowl and poured milk and sugar on it. That was either our breakfast or snack. When there wasn't anything sweet in the house, Mom spread butter on a slice of bread and sprinkled it with sugar.

For years, the groceries for our Thanksgiving and Christmas meals were provided by either St. Mark's or St. Cecilia's. When Mom couldn't afford to buy us Christmas gifts, she signed up for the donated Christmas gift program at St. Mark's.

One year our donated gifts still hadn't arrived three days before Christmas. I was sitting on the floor next to the gas heater when I overheard Mom calling St. Mark's to check on the status of her delivery. "But I've checked repeatedly, and they're not here. Are you sure you delivered them?"

The person on the other end of the line must have given an affirmative answer because Mom continued with panic in her voice, "Maybe they were delivered to the wrong address. Don't you have something you can send?"

The person must have told Mom they would send something because she replied, "Okay, thank you so much. I'll keep an eye out for them."

Two days later our church made a second delivery of used toys. Even though a game had missing pieces, Mom was grateful we had something to open for Christmas. We never found out what happened to the original delivery.

One thing we did have during the winters was an abundance of snow. One steep hill about a half mile from our home was used for sledding. Since Mom couldn't afford to buy us a sled, Chrissy and I made our own from cardboard boxes. Curlers were another thing Mom couldn't afford to buy Chrissy and me, so she cut brown paper bags into strips, rolled up a section of our hair into each strip, then twisted the strips to keep them together. Once our hair was dry and the brown strips removed, our heads were full of curls.

As poor as we were, we were always clean. We owned a huge old wringer washing machine and dried our laundry on a clothesline outside our kitchen window. Mom always seemed to be cleaning, cooking, doing laundry, ironing our school uniforms, and starching our white shirts. She rarely had money or time to enjoy her painting hobby.

In my catechism class I continued to learn about God, Jesus, his mother Mary, and all the saints. I loved God and hearing the religious stories. The nuns also taught us about the holy sacraments of the Catholic Church, including baptism, confirmation, and holy matrimony. Chrissy and I made our First Communion and Confirmation while at St. Mark's. On Sunday mornings we walked to church while Mom stayed home with our younger brother Ed.

St. Mark's Church was physically connected to the school. A huge cathedral built in 1851, it boasted life-sized statues of Mary, Joseph, and other saints as well as a life-sized one of Jesus on a large cross. Both sides of the church were lined with enormous stained-glass windows, each depicting a scene from the day of Jesus Christ's crucifixion called the Stations of the Cross. Any little sound echoed throughout the cathedral's vast interior, including the click of my heels when I walked on the polished wood floor.

Once a week, one of the nuns would lead each class over to the church in single file to confess our sins. Once inside, she divided the class into two lines, each group assigned to a priest who waited for us inside their confessional booths. Each booth had a curtained entrance for the priest and another for the confessor. A seat on each side was separated by a panel. The priest would slide open a small window in the panel, exposing a screen through which he spoke.

Once a student confessed, the priest would absolve them of their sins and dole out their penance, typically praying a couple of Our Fathers and Hail Marys. If a student was really bad, their penance might be to pray the entire rosary.

The first time I stood in the confessional line, I could hear a priest named Father Kramer shouting at whichever poor soul was inside his booth. His tirade echoed through the cathedral, and in an instant the remaining students in that line, myself included, moved quickly and quietly over to the other line. The nun in charge immediately walked over and without a word separated the line again, forcing half of us back into Father Kramer's line.

I stood there in fear as my classmate exited the booth with a reddened face. One by one, those ahead of me in the line entered and exited, some in tears. When my turn came, I was thankful I couldn't think of anything to confess and relieved to have made it through confession unscathed.

Most of my teachers were nuns. I was petrified of some of them, especially after witnessing them crack their rulers on the knuckles of any student who misbehaved. I was fortunate not to ever receive such discipline. Between my fear of Father Kramer and some of the nuns, it was definitely enough to keep me on my best behavior.

Because of our poverty, I never felt like Chrissy and I fit in at school. Showing my green and white "free lunch" card to the cashier in the cafeteria was another daily humiliation that contributed to my already low self-esteem. To make matters worse, Chrissy and I had to walk three-quarters of a mile to school. During the long, cold winter months, the distance seemed like miles. I envied the other students as they drove by in the warmth of their family cars. I also envied other neighborhood kids because they all had their fathers.

Another thing I didn't like was the dress code on exam days. Each year the students were allowed to wear regular clothes on those days instead of the mandatory uniforms. Mom could rarely afford to buy new clothes for Chrissy and me, and the small selection I owned was so well-worn I chose to just wear my uniform. But instead of solving my problem, it gave me yet another reason to feel different.

CHAPTER FIVE

The Cat Burglar

The thief cometh not, but for to steal, and to kill, and to destroy.

—John 10:10(a)

More than three years had now gone by since we'd moved. We hadn't heard from my father since he'd vanished when Chrissy and I were six. I'd assumed he must be dead as I could think of no other reason he would have stopped visiting us.

The Christmas after I turned nine, I was in the living room when the phone rang. I could hear Mom yelling at whoever was on the other end of the conversation. A few minutes later, she called me into the kitchen. Tears were spilling down her cheeks.

She held out the phone to me while wiping her wet cheeks with her other hand. "Your father wants to speak to you."

"My father?" Stunned, I took the phone. When I heard a male voice on the other end of the line, I broke into tears. The sound of my loud sobs drowned out my father's words. Then I heard him begin to sob. By now Chrissy had arrived in the kitchen. Unable to get out any words, I handed the phone off to my twin.

"Don't call this house again and make our mother cry," Chrissy told my father angrily, "or I'm going to call the cops."

Then she handed the phone back to Mom, who continued to quarrel with my father. He eventually hung up without telling Mom where he was or how we could get in touch with him.

During all these years, we'd had no contact with any of Mom's family. From time to time she spoke of how her family was separated when she was a child. To me, it seemed strange that she didn't know the whereabouts of her family as though she'd dropped from the sky with no family connections or roots.

But while we didn't know any relatives on Mom's side, some of my father's siblings kept in touch with us. Aunt Irene lived with her husband and daughter in a small house about thirty minutes away. Chrissy and I would occasionally take turns visiting on weekends to hang out with our cousin Sandy, who was our age.

Aunt Evelyn still lived in New York City and worked as a catalog model. To me, she looked like a movie star with her glamorous hats, oversized sunglasses, tiny figure, and latest New York fashions. She had met and married Benny, twenty years older and the owner of a women's shoe store in the City. For several years, Aunt Evelyn and Uncle Benny made the long drive upstate over the Christmas holidays to visit us and bring us gifts of toys and pajamas. One Christmas they gave us our first television.

Uncle Murray, who had lent my parents the down payment for their previous home, lived about thirty minutes away and no longer kept in touch. Occasionally, we would hear from the youngest sibling, Uncle Ron, who lived in Massachusetts. Still single, he looked like a cowboy in his ten-gallon hat and boots, topped off with a foul-smelling cigar.

My father's brother Norman had served in the Korean War and married shortly after being discharged from the army. He painted houses for a living and operated a coin business on the side. Even after my father left, he continued to visit us, which Mom appreciated since we had no father figure in our lives.

Uncle Norman reminded me of a cat burglar with his slim physique and the all-black attire he liked to wear. He kept his short, black hair coiffed to perfection with a small black comb that was a staple in his right back pocket. A sterling silver ring engraved with the image of St. Anthony, a thirteenth century Catholic priest known for his dedication to the poor, decorated his right ring finger.

I was nine when Uncle Norman divorced. He moved into a small efficiency apartment at the back of a tiny shop he'd rented nearby for his business. He often took us out to eat, for ice cream, or to the drive-in movie theater. Sometimes he would take just me with him to his shop or on outings to other coin dealers.

We would be gone at times for hours, and what no one knew was that Uncle Norman had started to sexually abuse me. The various depraved acts didn't include rape, but still made me feel confused, betrayed, and full of fear. Because of that fear, I kept his horrible secret. I felt helpless and lost.

When I was eleven, Uncle Norman announced that his house-painting business was failing and he could no longer afford his apartment. He asked Mom if he could pay her room-and-board to live with us. Since Mom considered Uncle Norman family, she took him in. For her this was a win-win situation since the extra income was much needed. He brought his own single bed and shared my younger brother Ed's bedroom.

Uncle Norman was a big help to Mom, paying his room-and-board every week and continuing to treat us to an occasional drive-in movie or ice cream. When Mom started dating a mechanic named Ray, Uncle Norman would babysit us on Saturday nights so Mom and Ray could go out. Sometimes Chrissy would be at our cousin Sandy's for the weekend, leaving Ed and me home alone with Uncle Norman. Or I would be the one at Sandy's while Chrissy was home. For some reason, Aunt Irene only invited one of us at a time.

Uncle Norman also made Chrissy and me vanities for our bedroom. Cutting pieces of plywood for the tops, he painted these and installed legs onto them, then bought pink fabric for me and blue fabric for Chrissy to make ruffled skirts around the vanities. I used my vanity for years to do my homework.

To my mother, Uncle Norman appeared to be someone she could trust around her children. He was funny and acted like a big kid. Mom treated him as if he were her younger brother. No one would have suspected him of any illicit behavior, and Mom was totally unaware that he was sexually abusing me.

Similarly, I displayed no outward manifestations that I was a victim of sexual abuse. To all appearances, I was the same shy little girl I'd always been. I loved to study as it took my mind off the negative things in my life, and I continued to earn good grades.

But along with the low self-esteem triggered by poverty and my father's abandonment, I had begun to feel dirty, ugly, and shameful. I didn't realize at the time that this was connected to the sexual abuse. Typical for a victim of sexual abuse, I kept those negative emotions and dark secrets locked deep inside.

Chapter Six

Tango

No weapon that is formed against thee shall prosper.

—Isaiah 54:17(a)

I was twelve years old that freezing February afternoon when I decided to buy Mom a Valentine's Day card to go with the box of chocolates I'd already purchased. Finding her in the kitchen, I asked, "Mom, is it okay if I walk to the store?"

Seated in the living room, Uncle Norman heard my request and called out, "I'll take her. I need to go shopping anyway."

At this point, Uncle Norman was scheduled to move out within two weeks.

Mom's boyfriend Ray had told her it was time Uncle Norman found another place to live, and Mom had agreed. She'd given Uncle Norman to the end of the month to move out.

As I climbed into Uncle Norman's grey and white Pontiac, I saw a box of rat poison on the back seat. I didn't find this unusual since we occasionally used it as well as mouse traps to get rid of mice.

"I need to make a few stops first," Uncle Norman told me as I settled myself into the front seat beside him.

The first stop was to a liquor store. I sat in the car while he went inside. A few minutes later, he walked out with a brown paper bag. I could see the neck of a bottle poking out the top of the bag. After he placed the bag on the back seat, we drove on. He smoked nonstop and hardly said a word. I sat beside him quietly, my usual introverted self.

Twenty minutes later our surroundings became much more rural with only an occasional house, farm, or business. Snow was piled high on both sides of the road from recent storms. The road signs indicated names of small towns I'd never been to, though I'd heard of some of them. I wondered where we were headed.

We continued driving on the same road until suddenly the car slowed down. That was when I noticed the bright neon sign of a motel next to the road. The motel was just one story with about a dozen rooms. Turning into the parking lot, Uncle Norman pulled up to the front of the motel and turned off the engine.

Why in the world would we be stopping here? I asked myself. *Well, maybe he's here on business.*

Taking the car keys, Uncle Norman told me to stay in the car. Then he walked towards a door displaying an "Office" sign and entered. As Uncle Norman disappeared through the door, I hoped he wouldn't be gone too long. With these frigid temperatures, I would soon be cold.

Looking around, I counted two other cars in the lot parked near the office, but saw no actual people during my wait. A few minutes later, Uncle Norman emerged and got back in the car. He drove down to the far end of the motel and parked in front of room number twelve.

Climbing out, he reached into the back seat and gathered some items. "C'mon. We're going inside."

In the three years that Uncle Norman had sexually abused me, he'd never taken me to a motel. Frightened and confused, I followed him inside, my heart pounding rapidly.

Uncle Norman locked the door behind us and turned on a small television sitting on top of a dresser.

I felt helpless as I sat in the room's only chair and gazed at the black and white images on the screen. I heard the rustle of the brown paper bag as he removed the bottle. Then I smelled the alcohol as he poured himself a drink. Just as in the car, he barely spoke a word in all this time. Suspecting what he had planned, I couldn't pay attention to the television program.

After he'd downed a couple of drinks, he made me undress and attempted to rape me. Thankfully, he was impotent. It was an enormous relief when the lengthy assault ended. I assumed we would soon leave. Instead, Uncle Norman grabbed the liquor bottle and poured another drink into a second glass. The label on the bottle read *Tango*, which was a cheap orange-flavored vodka.

I tried not to stare at Uncle Norman, but my peripheral vision caught him pulling a small box from the same paper bag that had held the liquor bottle. It was the box of rat poison I'd noticed earlier. Filled with dread, I watched as he took a little packet from the box. Tearing it open, he poured the powdery substance into the second glass of Tango. My panic level escalated.

"Here, drink this!" He handed me the glass as if its contents was medicine to make me feel better.

"I don't want to drink that." I couldn't understand why he would ask me to do such a thing. *Is he insane?* "I want to go home!"

"Drink it!" he ordered more harshly.

Grabbing my arm, he pushed the glass to my mouth. His olive features were engorged with rage and his dark eyes emanated pure evil as he forced the vile tasting liquid down my throat. I felt as though I were staring up at the devil himself—and I wasn't even sure there was one!

For years Chrissy and I had watched the horror movies that aired on television Saturday nights. Each film was filled with monsters, vampires, or other scary creatures. We would make a large pan of popcorn and sit in front of the television, enjoying the frightful characters. Now I was looking into the face of a real live monster, devil, or whatever he was, and he was trying to kill me.

God please help me!

At that moment, I put my hand to my mouth and ran for the bathroom. With my head over the toilet, I knelt on the floor and vomited. In between heaves, I sobbed desperately. Uncle Norman had followed me. Grabbing my long hair from behind, he held it away from my face.

Now he's concerned I'll get vomit on my hair? He's lost his mind!

But I didn't say a word out loud. I could only cry. I couldn't understand his insane behavior or figure out what had set him off. I certainly didn't want to say anything that would make him any angrier. Better to keep your mouth shut than to argue and make things worse was my motto. I hated conflict and avoided it at all cost.

Once my stomach settled, Uncle Norman told me to lie down and get some rest. In a state of psychological numbness, I obeyed. I was too frozen with fear to make a run for it. I thought about Mom and wondered again if she was worried about me. If she was, I knew there was no way she could find me.

Maybe this is all a bad dream, and I'll wake up and be in my own bed!

I kept my eyes opened as Uncle Norman paced back and forth. Suddenly, he snatched up one of the pillows. Getting on top of me, he pressed it down over my face. A rush of adrenaline ran through my veins as I grabbed at his arms to pull them away with all my strength. At the same time, I pressed my feet against the bed to push my body up, trying to throw him off me. I was quite tall and filled-out for a twelve-year-old, but my strength was no match for a full-grown man. Struggling to breathe, I kicked and punched as I fought for my life.

Then just as suddenly, he stopped. Rolling away from me, he lay on the bed in a state of exhaustion. I sat up and moved to the edge of the bed, gasping for air. My nose hurt, and I could feel moisture dripping down my lips. When I wiped the moisture away, I saw that it was blood. I began sobbing hysterically.

Getting up, Uncle Norman grabbed a small towel from the bathroom and handed it to me. "Here, use this. Hold your head back and squeeze your nose."

Tilting my head back, I pressed the towel to my face, but my nose screamed in pain. Taking care not to touch my nose, I wiped away as much blood as I could. *Why is he doing this to me?*

Uncle Norman poured himself another glass of Tango as if this was just another day. Lighting up one of his Camels, he began pacing while he smoked. I watched his every move.

If Mom was here, she would rip you to shreds like a momma bear protecting her young! You wouldn't stand a chance!

But Mom wasn't here, and my situation seemed hopeless. I was trapped in a real life, never-ending nightmare with no chance of escape.

Guzzling down the rest of his drink, Uncle Norman grabbed his keys. "Let's go!"

CHAPTER SEVEN

Wrestling with the Devil

For we wrestle not against flesh and blood.

—Ephesians 6:12(a)

A s we got back in the car, I was relieved my nightmare was over and I was finally going home. But my heart sank as Uncle Norman pulled out of the motel parking lot. Instead of turning back the direction we'd come, we were heading on down the road. Any hope of seeing Mom evaporated in an instant. I didn't dare ask where we were going.

The area soon became even more secluded with woods and an occasional farmhouse. The yellow beams of the Pontiac's headlights illuminated embankments of dirty, encrusted snow piled high on both sides of the road.

Uncle Norman slowed down, then came to a complete stop. Backing up a few yards, he maneuvered the Pontiac into a large pull-off area on the right side of the road. This was almost completely surrounded by trees so that only the driver's side was visible to any passing vehicles. As he turned off the ignition, sheer terror flooded every part of my being. I was sitting alone with a madman in this dark, wooded area.

Suddenly, Uncle Norman reached over, wrapped both hands around my throat, and began to squeeze. My fingernails dug into my own skin as I tried to pry his hands away. When my attempts failed, I punched and scratched at his face as hard as I could. We fought so hard we ended up in the back seat, his hands still locked around my throat.

My strength draining and in total despair, I had a fleeting thought to end my torment by not fighting back. But my desperate need for oxygen kept me in survival mode. I kept punching and kicking with a vengeance until as suddenly as he'd grabbed me, he let go of my throat, collapsing into an exhausted slump.

Relieved, I grabbed my throat and gasped for air. I was shocked I had survived another of this madman's attacks. *Why is he trying to kill me?*

But like a recharged battery, he quickly regained his strength. With angry frustration, he ordered, "Get back in the front!"

Overwrought with fear, I obeyed while he slid into the driver's seat. Just then the yellow beams of a car's headlights approached out on the road. It was the first car I'd seen since we'd pulled over. If only they would stop and help me!

But the headlights were now disappearing on down the road. As darkness closed in again, I lost any hope of survival. Opening the driver's door, Uncle Norman looked over at me. "Lock your door."

I had no idea what he might be planning next, but he sounded like a man on a mission to kill his evasive prey. Too frightened to do anything else, I obeyed. Climbing out of the car, Uncle Norman walked around to the back, his black military style boots crunching on the frozen snow.

Then I heard the creak of the trunk being opened. Seconds later it slammed shut. Staring out the window into the dark woods, I considered making a run for it. But by this point I had become a robot, numbly carrying out my uncle's orders.

The devil you know is safer than the devil you don't know.

Uncle Norman climbed back into the driver's seat. Opening the door had turned on the overhead light. This revealed a long wooden handle of what looked like a hammer sticking out of the left pocket of his wool tweed blazer. Renewed terror gave me the impetus to finally attempt an escape. Scrabbling at the car door, I managed to unlock it. But by now Uncle Norman had grabbed me by the hood of my coat.

I swiveled towards him to get into a better defensive position. With his free hand, he pulled the wooden handle from his pocket. That is when I realized it was not a hammer, but a hatchet.

Screaming with horror, I tried to push his arm back. But it was too late. The blade cut into my left eyebrow. Turning to protect my face, I raised my arms to try to keep the hatchet away from me. A second blow slammed into my head, barely missing my left ear. I lowered my head to get it as far from the blade as possible, but a third blow gouged into my scalp.

I didn't know how much longer I could fight. But just when I thought my life was over, the hatchet fell onto the floorboard beside me. Lifting my head, I saw my uncle hunched over the steering wheel. Thankful though I was to be free, I couldn't understand why he had released me or why he was just sitting there. He seemed completely unaware of me as though listening to or looking at something I couldn't see. Only years later would I come to learn just what that was.

Taking advantage of his distraction, I grabbed the hatchet, opened the car door, and threw the hatchet out into the snow. Uncle Norman didn't even try to stop me. Still hunched over the steering wheel, he was now crying.

Why in the world is he crying? Stunned and bleeding, I didn't know what to do. I was terrified this horrendous nightmare wasn't yet over, but I was now too petrified and in pain from my wounds to even try to jump out of the car and run.

Mommy! I cried mentally.

A few minutes later my uncle stopped crying. Pulling a handkerchief out of his pocket, he wiped his eyes and cleared his throat. Leaning across me, he pulled the car door shut. Then he started the car and began driving again on down the road. Silence filled the car.

Now where are we headed?

CHAPTER EIGHT

Mirror, Mirror on the Wall

My God has sent his angel, and has shut the lions'
mouths.

—Daniel 6:22(a)

M y head hurt badly, and blood dripped down onto my left
eye. Over and over, I wiped it away, wondering where
my uncle was taking me next. The Pontiac slowed as we
approached a gas station with a small convenience store. There
were no cars at the gas pumps and only one parked in front of the
store. Uncle Norman pulled in around the far right end of the
building across from two doors marked Ladies and Men.

"Stay here," Uncle Norman ordered. "I'm going to get the
bathroom key."

He headed into the convenience store, taking the car keys with
him. I don't know if he thought I was going to take off in his car or
not, but at only twelve years old, I didn't even know how to drive.
Nothing he did that night made sense.

I was in such a severe state of shock that once again I didn't even consider trying to run away from the car. I just sat there dabbing at the blood trickling down my face, traumatized and scared to death. Uncle Norman was back within a few moments. "Let's go inside."

Grabbing my arm, he guided me toward the door with a Ladies sign above it. Unlocking the door, he ushered me inside, then followed, locking the door behind him. Catching sight of my bloody, disfigured image in the mirror, I became hysterical.

"M-o-m-m-y!" I screamed.

"Quiet down!" Uncle Norman ordered in a harsh whisper.

Somehow I managed to lower the sound of my sobs. I stared in horror at my battered reflection. My face and neck were covered with blood, scratches, and bruises. I had two black eyes, and my nose was swollen. The whites of my eyes were bright red from burst blood vessels. The gash running through the top of my left eyebrow had a loose piece of bloody skin hanging down.

My shoulder-length dark hair was also saturated with blood as were my blue-and-white winter jacket and light-blue turtleneck. My hands were all bloody, and my right ring finger was swollen.

Uncle Norman handed me a wad of paper towels. "Wash the blood off your face and hands."

My hands trembled and my entire body shook violently as I cleaned myself up the best I could, tears streaming down my battered face. *This can't be happening to me!*

The bathroom had a vending machine, from which Uncle Norman purchased a package of small bandages. As soon as I threw the bloodied paper towels in the trash, he applied a bandage to the gash over my left eye. He ignored the gashes hidden beneath my blood-soaked hair. I accepted his first aid, but I couldn't understand his sudden concern for my well-being.

Once he'd finished patching me up, he unlocked the bathroom door. He peeked outside to make sure no one was in sight, then grabbed my arm and escorted me back to the car. "Stay here while I return the key."

Still too petrified to run, I just sat there in the front passenger seat as he went into the convenience store, again taking his car keys with him. He was soon back. Continuing down the same road we'd been on since the motel, he eventually pulled into the empty parking lot of a fast-food drive-in. He parked next to a telephone booth, which was located a good twenty yards from the customer window.

"Stay here." Getting out of the car, Uncle Norman walked up to the customer window. He returned a few minutes later and handed me a bag of food and a soft drink. "Here, take this. I need to make a call."

Fast food would have been a real treat on any normal day. But now the smell nauseated me. Rolling down the window, I tossed out the bag of food and drink.

Lunatic! First he tries to kill me, then he wants to feed me. What a freak!

A few minutes later, my uncle was back in the car. He turned on the ignition but didn't start the car. Instead, he turned to face me. "I just spoke with the operator. There's a state police station a few minutes' drive from here. I'm going to turn myself in."

I was astonished but hesitant to get my hopes up. I was too frightened to ask why he'd made that decision or why he'd been trying to kill me. I just sat there in terrified silence as he ordered me not to tell the police, Mom, or anyone else the truth about what had happened. I was never to mention that he'd poisoned, smothered, and strangled me or that he'd beat me with a hatchet. As with his prior sexual abuse, I was not to mention the motel or sexual assault.

Still, he had to come up with some explanation for my obvious injuries.

"When the police or anyone asks you what happened, just tell them I took you for a long ride," he ordered sternly. "I pulled over and began beating you with my hands. Then I stopped and drove around looking for a phone booth to find the nearest police station to turn myself in. You're not to say anything else. Got it?"

"Got it."

"Promise you won't tell?"

"I promise I won't tell."

Putting the car in gear, he headed for the state police station.

CHAPTER NINE

Must Have Been a Fairy Tale

How long shall I take counsel in my soul, having sorrow in my heart daily?

—Psalm 13:2(a)

When I walked through the side door entrance to our flat early in the morning on that Valentine's Day of February 14, 1967, I was so grateful to be home. I felt like I'd been gone for days. That all my uncle had done to me, my time in the hospital examining room, and the interrogation at the police station had in fact taken less than fifteen hours just didn't seem possible.

As we entered the living room, my twin sister and younger brother were watching cartoons on the television. They both cried at the sight of my injuries and gave me big hugs. Tears flowing down her face, Chrissy told Mom, "I'm not going to school today. I'm staying home with Mary."

Mom burst into tears. I didn't say a word. I just wanted to go to bed and block out this entire nightmarish ordeal. I went straight to my bedroom. Opening my drawer in the dresser I shared with Chrissy, I pulled out the beautifully decorated red-and-white heart-shaped box of chocolates I'd purchased earlier. I handed it to my mom, who had followed me into the bedroom. "Happy Valentine's Day, Mom."

"Oh, Mary!" Mom sobbed, wrapping me close in her arms.

Only then did I collapse exhausted onto my bed. Within a few moments, I was sound asleep.

Later that morning, Mom came in my bedroom and woke me. "Mary, you have a visitor. I called St. Mark's and asked if one of the priests would come by to pray for you. Father Arnold is here."

I stayed in bed as Father Arnold anointed me with oil and said a prayer. Moments later, I was fast asleep again.

Meanwhile Mom had called the school, telling them I was badly injured from a fall down the stairs. Chrissy told the same story to our seventh-grade classmates and friends. There was no way for Mom to inform my father of what his brother had done to me as she still didn't know his whereabouts and hadn't received a call from him in three years. She called my father's other siblings, telling them how Uncle Norman had assaulted me. None of them could believe their brother was capable of such violence. Nor did they know how to reach my father.

For the next two weeks, I stayed home to recover while Chrissy brought me my assignments from school. I continued trying to figure out what I'd done to make Uncle Norman want to kill me, but I couldn't come to any conclusion. I hadn't told anyone he was sexually abusing me, so that couldn't be the reason. Mom and her boyfriend Ray assumed Uncle Norman had flipped out when he was asked to find another place to live. But that would hardly be a motive to take it out on me. Could he have simply wanted to shut me up permanently for fear of what I might say once he was out of the house?

Once my stitches were removed, I was finally allowed to wash my hair. Standing with my head under the kitchen faucet, I scrubbed my hair clean, then rubbed it dry with a red towel. That was when I saw the head lice now sticking to the towel.

"Mom!" I screamed in panic.

"It's only head lice," Mom told me calmly. "We're going to have to cut your hair."

I couldn't bear the thought, especially after having already lost patches where the hospital staff had cut around my wounds. "No, please don't!"

"All right. We'll try to get them out without cutting it." Mom treated my hair with a lice killer, then ran a lice comb through it until all the dead bugs were gone. I couldn't wait for those disgusting things to get out of my hair. We had no idea how I got lice since no one else in the house had them. Perhaps from that motel room since who knew what kind of people might have slept in that bed I'd been forced to lay on.

Meanwhile Uncle Norman had been charged with second degree assault. At first he pled not guilty, even though he'd already confessed to assaulting me. His bail was set for just five hundred dollars, and when he couldn't pay that, the judge waived the fee, releasing him under his own recognizance.

His public defender then requested that Uncle Norman be admitted to the local state mental hospital for evaluation as to his mental capacity when committing the crime as well as for making his defense. Two hospital psychiatrists determined he suffered from mental illness but not severe enough to classify him as insane or incapable of understanding his actions. He was released again, still on his own recognizance, and voluntarily admitted himself to a local Veterans Affairs (VA) hospital for further evaluation.

After several delays, Uncle Norman switched his plea to guilty. The judge ordered him to serve eighteen to thirty-six months in Clinton Prison at Dannemora, New York, but then suspended the entire sentence. My uncle was put on probation for two years, placed under the additional supervision of the VA hospital, and ordered to stay out of trouble. He never stated why he assaulted me.

While the authorities didn't know the true extent of Uncle Norman's crimes, his lack of imprisonment felt unfair. As far as we knew, he had a clean criminal record, but that still didn't seem to warrant the judge suspending his entire sentence. We assumed it was part of some plea deal, which made us all very confused and angry.

Once Uncle Norman had assaulted me, we didn't hear anymore from Aunt Irene, my father's and uncle's sister who had first introduced my parents, though their other sister, Aunt Evelyn, still called on occasion.

After the assault, I experienced a horrific nightmare where I was falling over a cliff. I kept falling and falling, helpless and headed for certain death. But before I hit the ground, I awoke with a jolt, my heart pounding rapidly, only to realize it was just a bad dream.

Unable to share my secrets with anyone, I felt isolated and engulfed in an intense loneliness, no matter the number of people around me. I determined to live my life as though the entire incident had never happened, unaware that this was an unhealthy coping mechanism.

My outward behavior appeared normal. The physical wounds had healed, and the only evidence of injury was a pinkish scar that ran through my left eyebrow. My broken nose had healed, and the scars from the other gashes were hidden beneath my hair. But the real wounds were deep inside. I had become emotionally numb, though no one seemed to notice—not even me.

Worse, I'd lost faith in God. What I'd been taught in religious school and once hoped was true no longer seemed real. I came to the conclusion that any God who loved me wouldn't have allowed my uncle to almost murder me. Therefore what I'd been taught about God must have been a fairy tale.

Either that, or God had forgotten about me.

CHAPTER TEN

Best Dressed

That if any would not work, neither should he eat.

—II Thessalonians 3:10(b)

T hat same year Chrissy dreamt that our brother Ed was going to die young. Six years old now with developmental issues, Ed had been diagnosed as retarded, and Mom had her hands full with him. She'd enrolled him in a special education program at a nearby public elementary school. A small bus picked him up at our home to take him back and forth from school.

After her dream, Chrissy took Ed by the hand, walked to St. Mark's, and asked to speak to one of the priests. A priest named Father O'Malley came out and introduced himself.

"My name is Chrissy, and this is my brother Ed," she introduced in turn. "I was wondering if I could speak to you alone."

"Of course. Ed can sit here in the waiting area while we talk." Father O'Malley led Chrissy into his office. "So how can I help you?"

"Well, my brother was baptized as an infant," Chrissy explained. "He's six now, and he's retarded. He hasn't made his First Communion, and I'm afraid he'll go to hell if he dies."

"Let me talk to him for a few minutes." The priest asked Ed some questions before returning to Chrissy. "You have no need to worry. Your brother is incapable of understanding sin. He's a very special child and will surely go to heaven if he dies."

This satisfied Chrissy about Ed's eternal soul.

Meanwhile, Mom continued her relationship with Ray, who worked as a mechanic full-time and also repaired cars on the side. I immersed myself in school work and finished seventh grade with good marks. Chrissy and I both helped Mom with household chores and taking care of Ed. Since our old wringer washing machine was now broken, this included carrying dirty laundry several blocks to the laundromat.

I finished eighth grade with good marks as well. When it came time to register for high school, Chrissy and I both wanted to attend public school but for different reasons. I thought I wouldn't feel so different if I went to a public school. It would also provide an escape from those dreaded confessions.

Chrissy wanted to go to the public school because she was sick of school uniforms and wanted to wear regular clothes. She also wanted a school with a bigger pool of boys since she wasn't interested in dating any of the boys at St. Mark's.

"Can we please go to public school next year?" we begged Mom. "We don't want to go to Catholic high school."

"I want you girls to have a Catholic education," she responded. "Besides, I can't afford clothes for school."

"We can buy our own clothes," we insisted. "We'll babysit and do odd jobs to earn money."

"But what about your religious education?" she protested.

"We'll go to church on Sundays, we promise. Besides, St. Mark's is planning on closing in a year, so we'd have to go to public school for tenth grade anyway."

"Let me think about it."

The next day we asked Mom if she'd made a decision. She was still thinking about it. We waited a few more days before approaching her again.

"Please, can we go to public school?" we begged.

"Okay," she gave in. "As long as you girls buy your own clothes and go to church."

"We will!"

As promised, Chrissy and I went to church every Sunday. Chrissy didn't mind as she still believed in God. But I'd lost my faith that God was real, so I attended only out of obligation.

We both got part time jobs after school as telephone solicitors selling coupon books. Popular for decades, these books offered coupons to various restaurants and businesses, resulting in a huge savings to the consumer. I also babysat on weekends, earning enough money to buy my own clothes and pay for my own school lunches.

But though I now wore new outfits to school, I felt no better off than when I was at St. Mark's. I was still painfully shy, hated school, and felt different from everyone else.

Meanwhile, Mom's relationship with Ray was deteriorating. On numerous occasions, he physically assaulted her while intoxicated. She never pressed charges, but after three years she finally ended the relationship. I was more than relieved he was out of our lives. Mom got a part-time job at a local restaurant, but she continued to struggle financially with just enough money to pay for the bare necessities.

At sixteen, I found a part-time clerical job at an insurance company. In addition, Chrissy and I were both hired by St. Mark's Rectory to help in the office and kitchen. We alternated our hours so we never saw each other there. I loved both jobs, especially the rectory, where I became good friends with the cook. She and her sister Dorothy would also hire me occasionally to babysit.

By now I was not only earning enough to buy my own clothes and pay for school lunches but was able to give Mom money each week and open a savings account. I learned to "squeeze a dollar out of a nickel," as the saying goes, and was quite good at it.

I was still sixteen when my father finally called again. I was so happy to hear from him. He was living in Houston, Texas, and this time he gave me his phone number and address so I could keep in touch.

Around this time, Chrissy and I became close friends with two brothers about our age, Michael and Stephen. We met them at St. Mark's when they were hired to paint some of the rooms. We would spend time together at our church's teen center or at their home. I envied them because they had both parents who also owned their own home. Their family seemed so normal.

Sometimes Michael, Stephen, or both would walk me home at night. If they wanted to come inside, I made them wait in the living room while I went into the kitchen and turned on the light to ensure there weren't any roaches around. If there were, I gave them a quiet whack with my shoe and got rid of them before I let anyone into the kitchen.

My favorite classes were business and secretarial. In my junior year, I was inducted into the National Honor Society and voted "best dressed" by my classmates. In my senior year, I received the Outstanding Business Student of the Year award. I excelled in my secretarial courses and won competitions against students in other area schools in typing and shorthand.

My younger brother Ed was doing well too in his special education classes. He became close friends with James Lewis, the neighbor who'd brought him home after his many escapes down the street. Married with two older children, James became a surrogate father to Ed. They spent hours together talking about everything under the sun.

The only time I allowed myself to think about my dark secrets was when Valentine's Day approached. Each time the holiday's eve arrived, I would count the years since the assault.

CHAPTER ELEVEN

Déjà Vu

By sorrow of the heart the spirit is broken.

—Proverbs 15:13(b)

T hough Chrissy and I were twins, our differences in personality and taste were increasingly obvious by the time we reached our teens. I was introverted while Chrissy was extroverted. We took different classes in high school and hung out with different friends except for Michael and Stephen. Chrissy was on various school committees, took drama, and starred in school plays. I just wanted to go off somewhere and hide in a hole.

Chrissy also dated throughout high school, while my only date was when a classmate, George, invited me to our senior prom. George was smart and a very nice person. While we never dated again, I was grateful he'd asked me to the prom.

I was also about ten pounds heavier than Chrissy, while she was a quarter-inch taller. But we were still able to wear most of each other's clothes, which led to fights since we were paying for them ourselves.

Our one identical feature was our voice. No one could tell us apart on the phone, not even Chrissy's boyfriend Max, whom she dated throughout most of high school. If I answered the phone when Max called, I would let him chat away before letting him know I wasn't Chrissy.

Upon our graduation from high school, Chrissy got engaged to Max and applied to a local university in pursuit of a bachelor's degree in business administration. My own success in business courses encouraged me to pursue secretarial work, so I applied to Katharine Gibbs, a prestigious business school with five locations along the East Coast that trained young women to become top executive secretaries.

I was accepted into the one-year advanced course at their Providence, Rhode Island, location and received a fifty percent scholarship. Since Katharine Gibbs didn't provide dormitories, the school gave me contact information for a female classmate who was looking for a roommate. Over the phone, we agreed that she would find an apartment for the two of us before classes started in August.

But despite scholastic accomplishments and hopes for a rewarding career, my self-esteem remained extremely low. I wore a mask of normality on the outside, but inside I still felt like a freak, constantly self-conscious and insecure.

A week before my scheduled departure to Rhode Island, a friend invited me to a nightclub just a few blocks from our home that featured local rock bands. I hadn't yet turned eighteen, the legal drinking age at that time, but my friend assured me I'd have no problem getting in. Sure enough, the bouncer waved me into the nightclub without asking for ID.

The bartender did ask for IDs for any alcoholic beverages, so I just ordered a soda. The club was packed, the band playing so loud we couldn't converse without shouting. Looking around for anyone I knew, I spotted Nate, a man in his thirties who worked at the local grocery store.

Recognizing us, he came over to chat. A few minutes later, he offered to buy us each a beer. I was still drinking mine when I noticed Mom walking right towards me.

"Oh, no," I sighed.

Mom looked furious. "You're not old enough to be in here. And who bought you that beer?"

"I did," Nate confessed.

"She's only seventeen," she yelled above the music. "I could have you arrested." Then she turned towards me. "Let's go!"

Mom lectured me all the way home. It was the first time she'd ever needed to discipline me, much less in public, and I felt so humiliated I just wanted to hide.

"How did you know where I was?" I finally managed to interject.

"I have my spies to keep an eye on you!" she responded. "I don't have to worry about Chrissy since she has Max. But I don't want anyone taking advantage of you."

By that point I was glad to be leaving town. Dorothy, sister to the rectory cook and one of my babysitting clients, offered to help me move. She rented a U-Haul trailer big enough for my bed, a small desk, chair, and clothes, which she hooked up to the back of her car. I said my goodbyes to Mom, Chrissy, and Ed, and off we drove to Rhode Island.

The apartment my new roommate had rented for us was within walking distance of the school. The upper floor of a two-story house, it had two bedrooms, bath, kitchen, and large living room. The bottom floor housed a doctor's office.

My first week at Katharine Gibbs, a teacher asked to speak to me after class. When we met, she informed me my dresses were too short to meet the school's dress code. Mini-skirts and dresses well above the knee were the style then, but not for executive secretaries. I would need to buy new clothes or lengthen my hems. Unable to afford a new wardrobe, I chose the latter.

To help pay my bills, I found a part-time job at a travel agency located downtown inside Providence's historic Arcade Building, built in 1828. I enjoyed walking up the wide granite steps past beautiful Greek revival columns, and my boss was a true gentleman. Any time he needed me to work late, he would drive me home in his beautiful metallic-blue Porsche so I didn't have to wait for the bus.

Not bad for a girl who grew up on welfare! I would tell myself.

Now that I was away from home, I no longer attended church. It never even occurred to me to find one. School, work, and mounds of homework kept me busy. My roommate and I didn't socialize, but I became good friends with an outgoing young neighbor named Jean who would play a significant role in my life over the coming years.

One day I placed a call to the phone number my father had given me in Houston, Texas. To my dismay, a recorded female voice responded, "The number you have dialed is not in service. Please check the number and dial again."

Thinking I must have dialed the wrong number, I dialed again, only to hear, "The number you have dialed is not in service . . ."

What in the world? Something must be wrong!

Dialing the operator, I discovered my father's number had been disconnected. I eventually found out that no one else in the family knew where my father had gone, not even Uncle Ron. It was a repeat performance of his disappearance when I was six. I felt hurt and betrayed.

I went home for the Christmas holiday and again in the spring to be maid of honor in Chrissy's wedding. Uncle Murray walked her down the aisle. Chrissy and Max bought a cute little house.

A month before my graduation from Katharine Gibbs, the Central Intelligence Agency (CIA), along with several other large companies, came to the school to recruit soon-to-be graduates. Their pitch of working for such a fascinating organization was alluring, and I was one of four students who applied.

The CIA recruiters flew us to their headquarters in Northern Virginia for the testing process, my first airplane trip. There I took a typing and shorthand test, a psychological test, a polygraph, and filled out a lengthy application regarding personal information and work history. We were told a background investigation could take up to six months before we found out if we were hired.

The week before graduation, my friend Jean invited me to a party thrown by an acquaintance of her boyfriend. When we arrived, I smelled what I assumed to be marijuana. Then I noticed several partygoers rolling what looked like tobacco inside cigarette papers. I'd never smoked pot before, so I grabbed a beer and went over to observe what they were doing. Several joints were being passed around. Not wanting to admit I'd never done this before, I accepted one.

It didn't take long before I began feeling strange. The marijuana impaired my thinking and made me more self-conscious. I wanted to go home, but Jean wasn't ready to leave. Overhearing our conversation, another male guest offered to give me a ride. On the drive home, he pulled over and sexually assaulted me. I tried to make him stop, but I didn't stand a chance against his large, husky frame. He made me feel like that helpless twelve-year-old girl all over again.

Once again, I didn't tell anyone what happened. He never threatened me not to, so I don't know why I was too frightened to tell, though I'm sure now it was related to the abuse I'd suffered as a child. I never saw the man again, but the assault left me feeling like a magnet for abusers.

The following week I graduated with honors. Mom was working two part-time jobs at this point and took an advance on one of her paychecks to buy a bus ticket from New York to Rhode Island for my graduation. I packed up, and Dorothy moved me back home.

But I was no longer the same person. Up to this point, the worst thing I'd done was indulge in a little alcohol and pot. In fact, I'd been teased for years about being a little Miss Goody Two Shoes. I'd struggled hard to keep buried the memories of Uncle Norman's assault and childhood abuse.

But the accumulation of all I'd endured finally broke me, and this fresh assault along with my father's second disappearing act became the proverbial straw that broke the camel's back.

CHAPTER TWELVE

Filling the Void

A broken spirit drieth the bones.

—Proverbs 17:22(b)

That summer, Ed's doctor informed Mom that Ed didn't suffer from retardation but a form of autism, later defined as Asperger's. He progressed from special education classes to regular middle school classes, though two years behind schedule.

I found a secretarial job at a small private school with intentions of keeping it just until I was offered a position with the CIA. I gave Mom money each payday and saved for a car. Chrissy was still attending St. Mark's with her husband. One day when she'd invited the family over for dinner, she asked me, "Why don't you come to church with me on Sunday?"

"The roof would cave in if I did," I responded derisively. "Anyway, I'm just not interested anymore."

In truth, I'd continued to doubt God's existence since the Valentine's Eve assault. The only way Chrissy could have gotten me to church was if she literally dragged me.

Some of my former friends had gone away to four-year universities while others just drifted apart. But I made new friends with some of my co-workers. I didn't tell Mom that I was going out to nightclubs with them, even though I was now old enough to drink legally. One day a friend talked me into smoking a cigarette, something I'd never thought I would do. I choked on the smoke but enjoyed how relaxed it made me feel, and I was soon smoking a pack a day.

My friends also offered me pot. Though I didn't even like it, I smoked it to fit in. My new friends all lived this lifestyle, and it seemed a natural thing to do.

Chrissy was not interested in the bar scene or pot. She told me she'd tried pot, but it made her hungry and tired. She didn't want to get fat and lazy, so she never tried it again.

It might have helped if I'd been busier. For the first time in years, I didn't have piles of homework to occupy my evenings. With too much time on my hands, loneliness became a significant part of my life. I was around people at work, lived home with Mom and Ed, visited Chrissy, but it just wasn't enough. Though I was extremely shy, I longed for male attention. A boyfriend might fill my emptiness and take away the pain from my childhood.

I accompanied my friends to the clubs, hoping I would meet someone. But I didn't know how to dance and was petrified I'd be asked. So I would guzzle a few drinks to bolster my courage. The alcohol worked wonders, not only bringing me out of my shyness but making me forget my dark secrets.

Shortly after I turned nineteen, I ran into a former co-worker, Scott, at the grocery store. He was tall, handsome, and six years older than me. We hadn't seen each other since we'd worked together at an insurance company when I was in high school. He had since graduated from community college and was still working at the insurance company.

He asked me to go out with him, and we began dating. I was still living with Mom and Ed in the same old flat. Ashamed of our worn-out furniture and petrified he might see a cockroach, I never invited him inside when he came to pick me up.

A few months later, I finally received the anticipated job offer from the CIA. Since I was dating Scott, I couldn't bear the thought of moving away, so I turned down the offer. But I didn't want to stay in my current job, which offered no chance of promotion and a minimal benefit package. I decided to take the New York State Civil Service exam for a stenographer position. I found the exam quite easy and was sure I'd scored well. For weeks, I checked the mail for my results. At last an envelope arrived with the appropriate return address.

Tearing it open, I informed Mom excitedly, "I got a hundred on my exam! I'm number one on the list in the entire state. That means I'll be the first one they call for an interview as soon as a position opens."

And indeed I did receive an offer almost immediately. The job required taking two buses each way until I saved enough money for the down payment on a brand-new red Mustang. But I found the work a wonderful escape mechanism and plunged myself into it.

I was also crazy about Scott, though I didn't know how to express my bottled-up feelings or let him get close to me emotionally. What I couldn't say with words, I made up in other ways. I sent him cards and baked for him, which he appeared to enjoy, especially after we smoked pot. Still, Scott always acted aloof, leaving me to wonder if he really cared about me or just found me a convenient companion for sex, pot, and alcohol.

Then after nine months, Scott's calls suddenly stopped without notice or explanation. Nor could I reach him when I tried to call. One night he finally answered the phone, only to tell me he was seeing someone else. The news exacerbated my brokenness, and I cried for weeks.

It was difficult to concentrate while my boss dictated long, complex documents. But eventually I was able to get through the day without crying. I didn't realize it at the time, but my heart was hardening, the wall around my emotions growing even thicker.

I decided that an apartment of my own would make me feel better. To afford it, I sold my beautiful one-year-old red Mustang and bought an old Volkswagen Beetle. I found a small one-bedroom apartment, bought all new furniture, and fixed it up just the way I wanted. But living alone only intensified my loneliness.

I'd been an avid reader since childhood. Now I discovered romance novels. As I escaped into fantasy worlds where the heroine is always rescued by Prince Charming, I fantasized that one day I'd find my own handsome prince who would rescue me from a world filled with loneliness.

One day a friend who worked for another state agency invited me to their annual picnic. She'd also invited her brother and introduced me to him. With his long blond hair, striking blue eyes, and deeply bronzed tan, Chad could easily have been a cover model for a romance novel.

"So what do you think of my brother?" my friend asked.

"He's gorgeous," I replied.

"Well, he thinks you're hot and wants to go out with you."

"He does?" Looking at Chad across the lawn, I couldn't understand why he'd be interested in me out of all the young women who probably flocked around him like rock star groupies. "Tell him I'm interested." *One hundred percent.*

I learned that Chad was seven years older than me and owned his own landscaping and woodworking businesses. The following weekend he called me, and we began seeing each other sporadically. But I never knew when I was going to hear from him. If he wanted to see me, he'd call at the last minute, usually to say he had some great pot or hashish he wanted to share with me. I felt more like an afterthought than someone who meant anything to him. But I was so lonely and desperate for male affection that I'd immediately drop everything to be with him.

Chad reminded me of Scott, though even more handsome, more charming, and more aloof. But I didn't let myself get as attached to him as I had to Scott. Which was just as well as in less than a year Chad's calls also stopped.

CHAPTER THIRTEEN

All Hell Breaks Loose

And be not drunk with wine, wherein is excess.

—Ephesians 5:18(a)

Holidays and some Sundays were spent with my family. But that still left me alone many nights in my apartment. To fill the intense loneliness, I often went out drinking with friends on weekends, always hoping to find my own Prince Charming.

When I drank, I became happy, extroverted, and free. As soon as I'd had enough alcohol to loosen up, I would join my friends on the crowded dance floor. Multi-colored strobe lights filled the room as we gyrated to the latest tunes. Whenever Gloria Gaynor's "I Will Survive" played, we sang along at the top of our lungs. For me, it wasn't just a song but my life's motto.

I also went out with co-workers after work for an occasional Happy Hour or to the ladies' nights some nightclubs offered with free drinks for women. I envied co-workers who had spouses to go home to or appeared to be in healthy relationships.

But I lost all common sense when I drank. On occasion I'd experience blackouts where I couldn't recall any details of the night before or how I got home. Early one morning, I awoke to find myself in the back seat of my friend Beth's car. The last thing I remembered was going out to a nightclub with her and her boyfriend Neil the night before.

Raising an aching head, I looked out the window to see an unfamiliar neighborhood. *Where on earth is Beth?*

I leaned over the front seat to honk the car horn over and over. Finally, Beth came running out of an apartment door and yanked the car door open. "Stop! Do you want to wake the whole neighborhood?"

"Why did you leave me in your car?" I yelled.

"You were so drunk Neil and I couldn't get you out."

"So you just left me?"

"There wasn't anything else we could do."

I straightened myself up. "Well, you could have done something. I would never do this to you. I would have dragged you inside if necessary."

Her expression showed no remorse. "Look, let me just go get my car keys, and I'll take you home."

I didn't speak to Beth for weeks after that.

Shortly after, I started dating a young man named Keith. Picking me up one evening, he told me he was taking me to a movie. He drove us to a small theater I'd never seen before. The marquee over the entrance had a triple X next to the name of the movie.

"Is this a porn movie?" I asked.

"Not really," Keith assured me with a grin.

"What do you mean, not really?"

"It's not like that. Let's just go inside."

I protested for several more minutes before he convinced me to give it a try. "Okay, but if it's porn, I'm leaving."

The movie was sparsely attended, and within a few moments naked actors filled the screen. I got up. "I'm not watching this!"

Though it was at least five miles to my apartment, I fully intended on walking home. But by the time I reached the street, Keith was right behind me.

"I thought you said it wasn't porn!" I yelled at him.

He just laughed. "I'll take you home."

I didn't hear from him again, but I couldn't understand why I kept attracting the same caliber of men. *Why can't I be in a normal relationship? Just once!*

Before dawn one Sunday morning, I was awakened by a policeman tapping on my car window. Looking out, I realized that I was parked next to a gas pump. *Oh, no! I know this officer! I must look a mess.*

Officer Hanks was the husband of a former co-worker I'd met several times when he stopped by our workplace. Motioning for me to roll down my window, he asked, "Are you okay?"

I tried to recall why I was in my car. I remembered going to a nightclub with Beth the previous night but couldn't remember anything after that. "I guess I fell asleep after I stopped for gas. I'm okay now. I live just a mile up the road."

"I'll follow you to make sure you get home okay."

"That won't be necessary." *Oh brother. I hope he doesn't tell his wife about this.*

"I insist."

I knew I wasn't getting out of this and was relieved when I got home.

Another evening, I went to a party with a male co-worker. As soon as we arrived, I could smell pot. Before long, someone passed me a joint. "This is pretty powerful stuff that will knock your socks off!"

Taking a few drags, I passed the joint to my co-worker. A few minutes later, I was passed another joint and then another. About an hour later, I was sitting next to my co-worker on a sofa.

"I can't see!" I whispered to him.

He just looked confused. "What do you mean, you can't see?"

"Keep it down. I don't want anyone to hear us," I hissed back. "I can't see. Everything is black. I need you to get me out of here."

It took me a few seconds to convince him I really couldn't see a thing.

"I can take you to the hospital," he offered.

"No! I want to go home," I insisted. "Just give me your arm and guide me out of here."

Luckily, we weren't far from the front door. As my co-worker led, I shuffled alongside. I could hear a few whispers from partygoers who must have been wondering what we were doing. My co-worker drove me home and stayed with me until my sight returned about an hour later. I came to the conclusion the pot must have been laced with something that caused this unusual side effect.

I never told my family about the chaos in my private life. Neither Mom nor Chrissy had any clue about what I was doing when they weren't around.

As for Ed, he'd grown into a tall, handsome young man who was Mom's pride and joy. At sixteen, he'd finally started high school and played on the football and track teams. With a photographic memory, he could recite historical data at a moment's notice, especially about the Yankees or oldies music. Always responsible, positive, and energetic, he served on numerous school committees and worked at the local Boys Club. But he still possessed the innocence of a young child and was different from everyone I knew. To me, he was like an angel on earth.

Meanwhile, I continued to go from one dysfunctional dating experience to the next. I still couldn't get close to anyone emotionally, and because I felt like damaged goods, I believed no decent, upstanding male would ever want me. I was simply incapable of a healthy, wholesome relationship with the opposite sex.

I couldn't seem to get ahead financially either, never in debt but just living from paycheck to paycheck. My used Volkswagen was always breaking down and cost a fortune to repair. When I bought another used car, the same thing happened. Any money remaining after I paid my bills was spent going out to bars and clubs with my friends.

One Labor Day weekend, I went camping with a fairly new friend, Janet, and her boyfriend, Sam. Some of Sam's friends had pitched a tent next to ours. We started a fire, cooked some hot dogs, and sat around drinking a few beers. Then Sam took out some pot, which we passed around. Shortly after, Sam's friends began passing something else around.

"What's everyone taking?" I asked Janet in a whisper.

"LSD," she said. "It's great."

I'd heard of LSD, a hallucinogenic drug commonly referred to as acid, but I didn't want anything to do with "hard" drugs. "No, thanks. I'll pass."

"You'll like it," Janet pressed.

"I'm not interested," I snapped.

By now I was the lone holdout. Leaning over, Sam asked, "What's going on?"

"Mary doesn't do acid," Janet said.

"Listen, you've got to do some," Sam said. "My friends here won't feel comfortable if you don't."

I felt like a helpless victim again just like when my uncle made me drink the poisoned Tango.

"I'll just give you a tiny piece," Sam whispered. "No one will know."

Tearing off a small piece of the paper containing the powerful chemical, he told me to put it on my tongue. Tears streamed down my face as I obeyed. The hallucinations lasted for hours, and there was nothing I could do to stop it.

CHAPTER FOURTEEN

Dust in the Wind

For dust thou art, and unto dust shalt thou return.

—Genesis 3:19(b)

T hree days later, I was back to work bright and early. At twenty-four years old, I'd recently received a promotion and was now secretary to Patrick Enunzio, department head in a large New York State government agency with over five thousand employees.

Patrick was stereotypically Italian in appearance with his dark, wavy hair, goatee, glasses, and husky build, and his raspy voice had a heavy Italian New York accent like a mafia don in the movies. But in personality, he was actually a big teddy bear, and I always felt his nickname should have been Teddy.

The kindest man I ever met, he always treated me with utmost respect and was genuinely concerned for my well-being. He was married with five children, and I considered them the luckiest children I knew. I so wished he was my father.

I loved my job and was quite good at it. In all the years I worked, I only called in sick once because of the flu. But my personal life continued down the same path of self-destruction. I continued to find myself in one bad relationship after another, but each ended after just a few weeks or months.

Meanwhile, my twin sister was not only working full time and going to school at night but teaching occasional religious instruction classes to public school students. She and Max bought a beautiful new home. She also found a cute small house for Mom to rent and moved her and Ed out of the apartment we'd grown up in.

At some point during this time period, I arrived one day at my office elevators, heading down to lunch. A moment later, a man I vaguely recognized arrived and pushed the "up" button. While I didn't know his name, I thought he might be a recent hire who worked in another department on my floor.

"Hi," he said with a grin as wide as the Cheshire Cat's in *Alice in Wonderland*.

"Hello," I responded doubtfully. *What's he so happy about?*

I wasn't in the mood for small talk, so I looked in every direction but his as we waited for the elevator. When one arrived going down, I got on alone and immediately forgot about the encounter. It would be two full years later before I learned just why he radiated such joy.

Not long after the elevator encounter, I was on my way to work with my car radio tuned in to my favorite rock station. "Dust in the Wind," a popular song by a group named Kansas, was playing. It didn't have a typical rock sound but was mellow with slow lyrics and stringed instruments in the background.

I'd heard the song many times before, but this time the male vocalist's haunting lyrics made me contemplate my own mortality:

> Don't hang on.
> Nothing lasts forever but the earth and sky.
> It slips away, and all your money won't another
>   minute buy.
> Dust in the wind.
> All we are is dust in the wind.

Is that all I am? I asked myself. *Dust in the wind? Am I just going to die someday and turn into dust in the wind?*

For the rest of the day, those words replayed in my head like a broken record. From then on, every time I heard that song I was tormented with the question of where I would go when I died. The idea that I would one day turn to dust and disappear forever was hard to accept. Thoughts of death and my own mortality haunted me.

My entire life felt as though it was spiraling out of control. I blamed Uncle Norman for my unhappiness. I hated him with a passion and fantasized about hiring someone to kill him. I didn't just want him dead. I wanted him to suffer as he'd made me suffer.

I actually visualized Uncle Norman with a rope tied around each limb and the opposite end of each rope tied to a different horse as was a common punishment for criminals in the Middle Ages. When the crack of a whip sent the horses galloping off in different directions, my uncle's limbs would be ripped from his body in a much-deserved torturous death.

Of course, I knew I could never really hurt anyone deliberately. The fantasy brought some satisfaction but also distressed me because I hated having such evil thoughts, even about someone as vile as my tormentor. On February 13th, I counted the years since the assault. *Twelve years.*

Feeling I could no longer suppress my dark secrets, I finally made an appointment to see a counselor. Ms. Samson mailed me paperwork to fill out in advance, including my purpose in meeting with her. As my appointment approached, I wanted to cancel but mustered the courage to go forward.

When I arrived, the waiting area was empty. Sitting down, I could already feel my heart racing. I was at the point of bolting out the door when a professional-looking woman came out to greet me. "You must be Mary. I'm Dena Samson. Come on in."

Following Ms. Samson into her office, I took a seat across from her desk. I could already feel the tears welling up. She asked me to tell her why I was there, even though I had written it in the paperwork.

"I . . . I . . . I." No matter how hard I tried, I just couldn't get the words out. Instead, I let out the most gut-wrenching wail I've ever heard. Then I felt anger surging up inside me against my uncle. *If it wasn't for Uncle Norman, I wouldn't be here.*

Ms. Samson just sat there in silence until I gradually calmed down. The tissue in my hand was soaked, so I fumbled in my purse for another to wipe the wet mascara from my burning eyes.

"Take your time," Ms. Samson assured me.

She sounded so calm and understanding. I wanted her to know what Uncle Norman had done to me so she could help me move on with my life and put it behind me. I wanted her to have all the answers I didn't have. Why was my life spiraling out of control? Why did I end up in the wrong type of relationships?

But it was extremely difficult to open up to a stranger, let alone share my deepest, darkest secrets. I sat there speechless for what seemed like hours. Panic set in, and I didn't think I could go through with it. *Maybe I should just leave?*

But my desire to break free from my painful past kept me glued to my seat. I realized if I didn't talk soon my hour would be up. Then it happened. The words exploded out of me like a volcanic eruption.

As soon as I told Ms. Samson what Uncle Norman had done to me, I felt worse. It was just too painful to deal with the reality of my secrets. As I walked out of her office, I believed I was doomed to a life of misery and vowed to never return.

CHAPTER FIFTEEN

Angelic Ed

The words of the pure are pleasant words.

—Proverbs 15:26(b)

A few months later, a co-worker told me her friend was getting married and wanted to sublet her apartment. I went to see it right away. The apartment was one of three in a large house located in an upscale neighborhood. Each apartment came with its own garage, but this was the only one with a fireplace in the living room. It was my dream apartment, and the rent was low, so I agreed to take over the lease and moved in the following month.

Right about this same time, my younger brother Ed was hit by a car. The impact flipped him over the hood, and he hit his head on the pavement. With little more than a scratch on his head, Ed didn't think he needed to go to the hospital. But Mom called me in a panic, and I drove him to the emergency room. The doctor on call x-rayed him and said he appeared to be okay.

A month later, Ed called me to ask if I was interested in ordering a set of salt and pepper shakers he was selling for a school fundraiser. Since I was putting every extra cent I had into decorating my new apartment, I declined.

The following Friday, Ed and a number of classmates traveled to attend the annual statewide convention of their high school's Key Club, a student-led service program sponsored by the Kiwanis organization that Ed participated in. I was spending the weekend at home to work on laying new linoleum flooring in my kitchen. Early Sunday evening, I received a hysterical phone call from Mom. "Ed's been rushed to the emergency room. We're at St. Luke's Hospital."

I raced to the emergency room. Chrissy and Max had already arrived as well. Mom tried to explain what had happened.

"Ed came home this afternoon. He seemed fine when he left Friday for the convention, but didn't feel well on Saturday and went to see a nurse. She just told him he was anemic and gave him some orange juice. He went to bed early tonight. I was watching television when I heard a strange noise from his bedroom like air coming out of a tire. I found him on the floor unconscious and called 911."

We sat there for a while in a daze, wondering what was going on. Then a nurse came into the main waiting room and guided us into a private area. A few moments later, two doctors came in, their expressions somber.

"We're really sorry, Mrs. Robarde," one doctor said. "When your son arrived, he didn't have a pulse. We did everything we could, but we couldn't restart his heart."

I felt as though I'd been hit over the head with a brick. In a daze, I heard someone crying out, "Not Ed, not Ed!" Someone else, probably one of the doctors, was murmuring something about an autopsy.

Ed's funeral was held at St. Mark's. The high school excused from class any students wanting to attend, and many student Key Club officers and members from around New York State who knew Ed also came. The cathedral was packed with family, friends, teachers, and classmates. Many shared their own special stories about Ed, his easy-going personality, infectious humor, and heart of gold. Others read poems or spoke about the fun they'd had together.

When the service concluded, Mom draped her body over Ed's casket and cried inconsolably, collapsing on the floor. I was still in a stunned state, just going through the motions like a zombie. I regretted not buying the salt and pepper shaker set he'd tried to sell me just days before his death.

Shortly after Ed passed away, Mom found an autobiography he'd written just seven days before his death. In it, he mentioned his family, his school, job, hobbies, and his goals of going to college to become an accountant. There was no mention of anything negative. That was Ed. Always optimistic.

The following month, Mom received Ed's autopsy report. It stated that Ed's cause of death was acute myocarditis, a rare condition that causes inflammation of the heart muscle. In most cases, there are no symptoms. Viral infections are a leading cause, leaving the heart damaged even after the virus clears up. But the report stated that there was no virus present in Ed's system. We wondered if the car accident just a few weeks earlier could have contributed to his condition, but no final cause was ever determined.

Ed's death was not only a great loss to our family and friends but to his school and community. A Humanitarian and School Spirit Award was set up in Ed's memory by the high school, and an annual camp scholarship in his name was awarded by the Boys Club to send two boys to camp each summer. The local newspaper wrote up a story honoring Ed's memory and the lives he touched. One of his teachers was quoted as saying "the only four-letter word Ed knew was love."

An intense sadness engulfed me after Ed's passing. It made no sense that this loving, angelic young man had just gone into the ground and that was the end of him. I was convinced he'd gone somewhere and came to the conclusion that this "somewhere" must be heaven.

But if heaven was real, then God was real.

And if God was real, I was in big trouble!

I felt I needed to get right with God for the unwholesome life I'd lived these past six years, but I didn't know how to go about it or if it was even possible. I felt doomed, empty, and alone.

Then just a few weeks after Ed's death, I had emergency surgery to remove a hemorrhaging cyst on my ovary. Here I was just twenty-five years old and having major surgery. It petrified me.

After my surgery, I had to stay in the hospital for seven days. I was moved into a room with another young woman who was undergoing treatment for cancer. A curtain was kept pulled to separate us, and since I didn't want to bother her with trivial conversation in her condition, we never conversed.

On the far side of the curtain, she either slept, screamed out in pain, or moaned. Each day hospital staff would take her to her treatments. And each day she begged for more morphine.

"You've already been given your limit for now," the nurse would say. "We can't give you any more for another hour."

As soon as they gave her the morphine, her screams and moans grew quiet. On the fifth day of my stay, she didn't return from her treatment.

"Where's my roommate?" I asked the nurse that evening. "Did she go home?"

"She passed away," the nurse responded simply.

"Oh no!" The news of her death so soon after Ed's exacerbated my thoughts about death and my eternal destination.

I'm next!

CHAPTER SIXTEEN

Not a Club

Marvel not that I said unto thee, Ye must be born again.

—John 3:6-7(b)

M om couldn't bear to live in the same little house where Ed had passed away, so we found her a one-bedroom apartment.

Two months later, Chrissy called me. "Why don't you join Weight Watchers with me? I want to lose the fifteen pounds I've gained since I got married."

"I don't know," I responded. "You know I'm not one for joining clubs."

"Well, you've been talking for years about wanting to lose ten pounds."

My twin was right. It wasn't a lot of weight, but those pounds seemed to stay right on my hips. I agreed to give it a try.

Once I learned the program, I didn't want to waste my limited calories on alcohol, so I quit drinking. But now that I'd stopped drinking, I didn't enjoy the nightclub or bar scene, so I lost all interest in partying with my friends. Since I wasn't out partying, I was also no longer interested in smoking pot, though I did continue smoking cigarettes.

In less than two months, I'd lost the ten pounds. Chrissy talked me into joining her as one of the models in a Weight Watchers fashion show at a local shopping mall. The following week, I was on my way to work with the car radio tuned in to my favorite rock station. The DJ was asking his daily trivia question. "What is the most widely read book in the world?"

That's easy! I told myself. *The encyclopedia.*

After the next song, the DJ announced the answer. "The most widely read book in the world is—the Bible!"

The Bible? Who in the world reads the Bible? I couldn't believe that was the answer. Even though I'd gone to Catholic school, I'd never bothered reading the Bible and didn't know anyone who did. I imagined it to be a tiresome, dull book filled with stories I'd learned from the nuns and priests.

A few days later, I noticed one of my co-workers carrying what looked like a Bible. He worked in another department, but I knew his name was Simon Woods. I was curious why he'd brought a Bible to work.

"Is Simon a preacher or something?" I asked another co-worker. "I thought I noticed him carrying a Bible."

"He's a Christian," she responded. "They have weekly prayer meetings in the building."

I wondered why anyone would want to attend a boring prayer meeting. Then a few days later, I received a call from Jean, my former neighbor in Rhode Island. We'd kept in touch over the years. She told me she'd become a "born-again" Christian. I'd heard the expression before but had no idea what it meant.

"How can someone become 'born again'?" I asked.

"It's like you're born all over again, but this time it's a spiritual birth," Jean explained. She was so excited to share her new faith with me. She went on and on about Jesus as though he was her new best friend. She explained how God would forgive us of anything we did wrong if we were truly repentant and give us a whole new start on life.

Even though I'd been feeling I needed to get right with God since my brother's death, I wasn't interested in hearing about Jesus. I'd never heard anyone talk about him outside of church or catechism class. It seemed fanatical. I wondered if Jean was involved in some type of cult.

"I'm already a Christian," I told her one day. "I'm Catholic. I was baptized when I was a baby and made my First Communion and Confirmation. I was taught about Jesus in Catholic school and even worked at my church rectory."

"A Christian isn't just someone who has head knowledge of Jesus," Jean insisted. "A true Christian is someone who accepts what Jesus did for them and accepts him into their heart. You can even have a personal relationship with Jesus."

"I'm not interested in joining any clubs," I told her with irritation.

"It's not a club."

"Well, I'm still not interested."

While Jean was trying to convert me, a former boyfriend called, wanting to get back together. I told him I wasn't interested. After Ed's death, I was no longer interested in the same unwholesome relationships I'd had in the past. I wanted to be in a normal healthy relationship, though this was foreign to me.

Jean's persistent phone calls to talk about God's love for me continued for months.

"I can't talk right now. I have to go," I'd cut her off. *How can God possibly love me, when he's obviously forgotten about me? Where was he when Uncle Norman was trying to murder me?*

As the holiday season approached, I was filled with a profound sadness. Ed's death intensified my emotional state. I decided to quiz Jean the next time she called.

"Can you wear makeup if you're a Christian?" My makeup was very important to me, and I couldn't imagine not being allowed to wear it.

"Yes, I wear mine."

"Well, then, what does someone have to do to become 'born again'?" My question was more out of curiosity than anything else.

"It's quite simple," Jean responded. "You admit to God you've sinned, acknowledge that Jesus died on the cross for your sins, and believe God raised him from the dead. Then you accept him as Lord and Savior. This is often called the 'Sinner's Prayer,' but it's a matter of sincerity of the heart, not any specific words you need to pray. This is called the message of salvation or the gospel."

"Then what happens?"

"Once you do this, the Holy Spirit comes to dwell inside you and you become spiritually reborn, or what is called 'born again.' God forgives your sins and erases them like someone erasing chalk from a chalk board."

"Is that it?"

"Well, to mature as a Christian, you should pray to God on a regular basis, read and study the Bible, go to church, and put biblical teachings into practice to develop a relationship with Jesus."

Jean was unaware of my sincere desire to get right with God, and for some reason, I was still resistant to what she was saying.

Throughout Christmas week, I tried to get into the holiday spirit. I decorated a Christmas tree and did some last-minute shopping. But the sights and sounds of Christmas made me feel worse. In hopes of lifting my spirits, I offered to host our family Christmas dinner, which was usually at Chrissy's or Mom's.

When Christmas Day finally arrived, I prepared busily for my family's arrival. But instead of lifted spirits, I was just anxious for the day to be over so I could put the holidays behind me. Even the aroma of sugar cookies in the oven didn't lift my somber mood. I plodded through my preparations with a heavy heart.

Then Mom called to say she was sick in bed and wouldn't be coming. Chrissy and Max eventually arrived. We ate dinner and exchanged gifts around the fireplace, but as much as we tried to be in a festive mood, Ed's death was on all our minds.

After Chrissy and Max left, I was overcome with sadness, loneliness, and emptiness. Climbing into bed, I buried my head in my pillow and sobbed. I could no longer hold back the intense emotional pain. I felt there was no hope that I could ever feel normal like other people. No hope I could share my life with a special someone in a healthy relationship. No hope anyone could undo the bad things that had happened to me.

Why did those horrible things have to happen to me? What did I ever do? I never hurt anyone. I wish I was never born!

Filled with self-pity, I couldn't shake the "why me" attitude that had burdened me for years. The hole in my heart felt enormous, and my entire twenty-six years of life felt shadowed by inescapable dark clouds. I reflected on my conversations with Jean over the previous months. The idea that God would erase my sins and allow me to start over with a clean slate seemed unimaginable.

Could it possibly all be true? I've been miserable for years. I need a new life. I wonder if this could be the answer. What have I got to lose?

For the first time in my life, I felt a glimmer of hope and wanted to pray. I cried out to God from the deepest part of my being. "Dear God, please help me!"

I was unsure if anyone was hearing me, but I had nowhere else to turn. "If what Jean told me is true, I want to be forgiven of my sins and start my life over. I'm so sorry for the bad things I've done. I believe Jesus died on the cross for my sins and that he rose from the dead. I willingly turn away from my former lifestyle and ask Jesus to become Lord of my life from this day forward. From now on I want to follow your plan for my life."

Jean had said we were to end our prayers with the name of Jesus, who daily sits at the right hand of God the Father and makes intercession for us. She'd explained that Jesus is the mediator between God and us. So I added, "In Jesus's name, amen."

In that moment for the first time I could remember, peace came over me. I drifted off to sleep.

CHAPTER SEVENTEEN

A Different Lens

And the disciples were called Christians first in Antioch.

—Acts 11:26(b)

T he next morning I noticed the incredible weight I'd carried around my whole life had been lifted off my shoulders. In addition, I felt a peaceful presence around me I couldn't explain.

I had an extra day home because of the Christmas holiday, so I settled down to read the newspaper with my morning coffee. As I reflected on my previous night's decision, I felt a desire to read the Bible and was disappointed I didn't have one. Then I remembered that someone had given me a pocket-sized New Testament when I was a teenager. I'd never read it, but I was sure I'd saved it.

Rummaging through a storage trunk in my bedroom, I finally found the New Testament underneath a bunch of old letters and scrapbooks. It started with the Gospel of Matthew, which told the story of Jesus's birth, life, death, and resurrection. The words brought comfort as I read for hours.

That night I called Jean to tell her my good news. Excitedly, we made plans for me to visit her after the holidays. Then she asked, "Do you own a Bible?"

"I have a New Testament."

"You need to buy a Bible. It will have both the Old and New Testament in it."

I went to Kmart the next afternoon. I'd assumed there would only be one option, so I was overwhelmed when I saw Bibles in various sizes and versions. *Ugh! Jean didn't tell me which one to get!*

I finally settled on a medium-sized King James Version with a white zippered leather cover. I began reading it that night, and I couldn't put it down.

The Sunday morning after Christmas, I was scanning through television channels when I saw B.J. Thomas, a famous pop and country singer whose music I enjoyed for years. He was being interviewed by a minister on a Christian program. During the conversation, he talked about how he'd recently become a Christian after struggling for years with drugs and alcohol, which was news to me. He seemed to have a peace about him. A peace I'd longed for my entire life.

The minister asked him if he would sing for the audience. B.J. sang one of his recent hit Christian songs. The lyrics spoke directly to me just like the day I'd heard "Dust in the Wind" on the radio. It made me want to have the same close relationship with Jesus I could see B.J. had.

The following morning on the way to work, everything looked different. The sky was bluer, and the clouds appeared as though painted on a canvas. I wasn't one to marvel at nature's beauty, so even noticing this was unusual. But then the atmosphere around me had always seemed so dreary before. I was now looking at the world through a different lens.

I took my Bible everywhere and read it several times a day, devouring the words like a starving animal given a plate of food. I could feel God's love pour off the pages in the New Testament. The Old Testament captivated my attention with its miraculous stories of God's intervention. Instead of the boring book I'd imagined it would be, it was filled with adventure, drama, romance, and war.

Two weeks later, I visited Jean and showed her my new Bible.

"You know the King James is the most difficult version to read," she told me.

"Well, I thought it was a little difficult, but I assumed they were all like that," I responded. "That's okay, I like it anyway."

The following morning, we went to church. It was my first time in eight years other than the occasional wedding or funeral and the first Sunday service I'd attended that was not Catholic. People were greeting each other with a handshake or a hug as they entered. They all seemed so cheerful and friendly.

I also noticed there were no religious statues. The only religious symbol I saw was a large wooden cross at the front. It was the first time I'd seen a cross in a church without Jesus hanging on it.

The service was also very different from the reserved services I'd attended in my childhood. The music was contemporary and upbeat. People sang in loud voices, clapped, and even raised their hands during parts of the songs. The pastor's sermon about God's plan and purpose for our lives gave me hope and encouragement.

Once he finished, the pastor asked if anyone wanted to commit their life to Jesus Christ. Anyone interested was invited to the front to accept Jesus as their Lord and Savior. I had asked Jesus to come into my life a couple of weeks earlier, but I wanted to do it again. I didn't know at the time that I only needed to do it once.

As I walked toward the front, I remembered Mom watching the Billy Graham Crusades on television when I was a child. At the time, I couldn't understand her interest in the show. It seemed so boring. At the end of his sermon, Billy Graham would ask anyone who wanted to accept Jesus Christ as Lord and Savior to come to the front of the platform to make their commitment publicly. Until this moment, I'd never understood why those people went forward.

Kneeling down at the altar, I broke into weeping. Years of pain began to pour out of me. It was a welcomed relief.

It was also just the beginning.

CHAPTER EIGHTEEN

The Palm of His Hand

Behold, I have graven thee upon the palms of my hands.
                                    —Isaiah 49:16(a)

Several days after I attended Jean's church, I called Mom. With excitement, I announced, "I've become a born-again Christian."

"That's nice," Mom said calmly. "I just ran into Dorothy Washington's brother. He told me he became a born again too."

"He did? I would love to talk to him."

I was anxious to meet another Christian in town. Mom and I looked up his phone number, and I called him right away. He invited me to his church, which wasn't far from where I lived. The service was a lot like Jean's church. I began attending twice on Sundays and every Wednesday night as well as various home Bible studies during the week.

Everyone at church and Bible study talked about Jesus as if they knew him personally and often referred to him as their Lord.

They spoke as if he was their best friend. I also sensed God's presence at this new church. I was told it was the Holy Spirit.

Any time the pastor asked if anyone wanted prayer, I raised my hand. But I was also learning to pray directly to God in a conversational style rather than the formal recitations I was taught as a child. I learned I could pour my heart out to God anytime, anywhere, and about anything. My prayers didn't even have to be spoken. God could read my mind. My faith grew as my prayers were answered. I now believed God wasn't a fairy tale as I'd come to believe after my uncle tried to murder me. God was real, and he loved me.

I also learned about adult baptism as an outward proclamation of one's decision to follow Christ. I'd been baptized as an infant, but now I made the decision to go public with my faith and get baptized by full immersion in water.

My faith was encouraged by a popular Christian television program called *The 700 Club*. It included commentary about national and world news, live interviews of famous Christians, music by popular Christian artists, and prayers for those watching. Each episode also featured a taped interview about God's divine intervention into someone's life. Those stories of dramatic conversions, miraculous survivals, supernatural healings, restoration of marriages, and other incredible testimonies encouraged me and built up my faith.

When I shared my new faith with Chrissy, she couldn't understand the dramatic change in me. She was furious that I, who had smoked pot, been involved in sexual relationships outside of marriage, hadn't gone to church for years, and still smoked cigarettes, was telling her what it meant to be a Christian.

"I'm already a Christian," Chrissy told me just as I had previously told Jean. "I believe in Jesus, go to church, have taught religious instructions, and help the poor."

"Being a Christian means we base our salvation on what Jesus did for us, not what we do for him," I replied. "I thought I was a Christian too just because I was a Catholic. But belonging to a specific denomination doesn't make us a Christian either. I know now that God is real, and I have a personal relationship with him."

Chrissy figured I must be involved in some type of cult. It reminded me of my conversation with Jean when she first tried to talk to me about what it meant to be a Christian. Instead of arguing, I decided to just pray for her and be an example. In any case, Chrissy was such a gifted speaker I figured I had no chance if we got into a debate.

Despite Chrissy's reaction, I was excited about my new faith and wanted to share the news with others. When I told my boss, he told me he'd noticed a change in me.

I couldn't think of anyone else to tell at work until I remembered Simon, the co-worker I'd seen with a Bible. Heading for his office, I found him sitting at his desk. Tapping on his door, I blurted out, "I was told that you're a Christian."

He smiled at me. "I am."

"Well, I wanted to let you know I just became one."

"Congratulations!"

"Thanks," I said. "I'll see you around."

Less than an hour later, a man showed up at my desk. I was surprised to recognize him as the co-worker with the big grin I'd run into once waiting for the elevator.

"Hi, Mary," he said, his beaming smile once again as wide and toothy as the famed Cheshire Cat's. This time he introduced himself. "My name is Arthur, and I work in the personnel department."

"Yes, I've seen you around the office," I responded politely, unsure why he'd approached me.

"I heard you became a Christian. I'm also a Christian, so I just wanted to offer my congratulations."

I could see he was genuinely excited about the news, and I immediately brightened up, giving him a big smile of my own. "Yes, I did. I'm so glad to meet you."

"Well, I just wanted to let you know there are other Christians who work in this building. We meet at noon on Wednesdays for prayer if you're interested."

"Oh, yes, someone told me about that. I'm definitely interested."

It was such a relief to know there were other Christians at work. Over the next few weeks they showed up at my desk to introduce themselves. They were evangelical, Baptist, Pentecostal, Catholic and other denominations. They seemed to have a peace about them like the other Christians I'd met at my new church.

The first Good Friday after I became a Christian, I attended a church service a few blocks from my office. As each person arrived, they were greeted and handed a laminated bookmark with the sculpted image of a little girl nestled in a large hand. Tears filled my eyes as I read the words below the image, an excerpt from Isaiah 49:15-16: *"I will not forget you! See, I have engraved you on the palms of my hands."*

At that moment I knew God was speaking directly to me. It wasn't an audible voice but a quiet inner voice that told me he hadn't forgotten me after all. The very night my uncle had tried to kill me, God had extended his mercy to me. He was the reason I survived. There was no longer any doubt in my mind.

From that moment on, I no longer blamed God for allowing the murder attempts to happen, and I no longer felt like a freak. Instead, I felt extremely special, extremely grateful, and freed from the "why me" attitude I carried for years.

CHAPTER NINETEEN

A New Creature

And be not conformed to this world, but be transformed
by the renewing of your mind.

—Romans 12:2(a)

I n one of my conversations with Arthur, I mentioned how I'd
become a Christian through a friend and how I'd learned that
we can ask God to send Christians across the paths of non-
Christians to tell them how much God loves them and to tell them
about Jesus. As I finished, I added, "I wonder if anyone prayed for
me."

Arthur looked at me with his usual ear-to-ear smile. "I did."

"You did? But you didn't even know me. Why did you pray
for me?"

"I don't know if you remember running into each other one
day at the elevators," he said. "It was a good two years ago. You
were going down and I was going up, so we didn't get on the
same elevator or even talk. But I sensed a deep sadness about you
and felt God wanted me to pray for you. When I got home that

night, I told my wife about it. That's when we started to pray for you. I almost fell out of my chair when Simon told me you'd become a Christian."

When I thought about what he'd said, I realized his prayers had initiated the turning point in my life and all that had transpired in the past two years he'd been praying for me. It all made sense now as to why I was haunted with thoughts of death by the song *"Dust in the Wind."* How I'd finally gone to a counselor to try to deal with what my uncle did to me. How I'd started wondering where my brother went when he died. How I'd wanted to change my lifestyle. How I'd stopped going to bars and given up pot after I joined Weight Watchers. And finally, how God had used Jean to tell me how I could get right with him.

Once again, I was astounded at how God had extended his mercy towards me when he specifically asked Arthur to pray for me. It made me feel even more special. I became good friends with Arthur and his wife Ann. They invited me over for home prayer meetings and occasional dinners at their house, where I met their four adorable young sons.

A couple months later, I met Welder at one of my Bible studies. He was also a fairly new Christian. Tall with light-brown curly hair, he was eight years older than me and worked as a welder. Both of his arms were covered in inked images of an anchor, an American flag, a skull, a coiled snake, and a Harley Davidson. We saw each other at church and Bible study and sometimes went together to his parents for dinner.

"I used to be in a motorcycle gang after I got out of the Navy," he told me one evening at Bible study. "I was quite wild in those days."

"I can't picture you in a motorcycle gang," I said as I looked at his arms. The tattoos all made sense now. "You must have really changed."

Welder and I always prayed together when we saw each other. Though we hadn't known each other long, he became like a brother to me. Then Welder was tragically killed in a car accident. This came as quite a shock and shook me up for weeks. My one consolation was that I knew he was in heaven.

The more I read and studied the Bible, the more God used his Word like a supernatural hose to wash me from the inside out, softening my hardened wounded heart and healing it layer by layer. It was a manifestation of Hebrews 4:12 as though God's Word was performing surgery on my spirit:

> For the word of God is quick, and powerful, and sharper than any two-edged sword, piercing even to the dividing asunder of soul and spirit, and of the joints and marrow, and is a discerner of the thoughts and intents of the heart.

My very facial features became more relaxed, and like "Cheshire Cat" Arthur I now always wore a smile. I received many compliments about the new sparkle that had replaced the old deadened aspect in my eyes, and the difference in my photos after I became a Christian was palpable.

The change in my appearance was noticeable at work. I was happy and upbeat all the time and could sense that many of my co-workers were wondering what had happened to me. Certainly if my co-workers had ever voted for the employee least likely to become a Christian, I'm sure I'd have made the short list.

One of the biggest differences in my life was my new ability and eagerness to talk about what my uncle had done to me. This usually occurred when I was at church or Bible study. Once I shared my secrets, it released me from the shame I'd carried for years. For the first time in my life, I was also no longer paralyzed with fear of the consequences if I told. The more often I told, the easier it became. As I broke the vow of secrecy, it became a part of my emotional healing.

I was now living in a different world as though an invisible hand from heaven reached down and pulled me out from a world of darkness into a world of light I never knew existed. I felt a completely different person. Same name. Same body. Different spirit. Different thoughts. Different actions. As it says in II Corinthians 5:17:

> Therefore, if anyone is in Christ, he is a new creature; the
> old has gone, the new has come.

"I wonder why no one ever told me before that I could have a personal relationship with Jesus," I asked one of my new Christian friends.

"Maybe they did, but you weren't interested," she responded.

I wondered about that. Was I told and just wasn't interested? It was quite possible. For six months Jean had talked to me about Jesus, but I'd thought she was in a cult and tried to avoid her. Either way, I wished I had discovered this new relationship years earlier before my life spiraled out of control. My life would have been a whole lot better if I had.

But, I was happy that God had forgiven me for my past and given me a second chance. Now I wanted to do all he required of me.

Chapter Twenty

A Nun or Something

Forgive, and ye shall be forgiven.

—Luke 6:37(b)

T he more I read the Bible, the more its message of forgiveness stood out to me. The parable Jesus told in Matthew 18:23-35 of the unmerciful servant was one story that truly affected me.

The parable tells of a king who wanted his servants to settle their unpaid accounts. One servant owed a large sum of money but was unable to pay it. The king ordered that the man, his wife, children, and all he owned be sold to repay the debt. Falling on his knees, the servant begged the king for more time to repay what he owed. The king had mercy on his servant, cancelled all of his debts, and let him go.

The servant promptly went out and located a fellow servant who owed him a small sum of money. He grabbed the man and choked him, demanding he repay his debt. The fellow servant fell on his knees, begging for more time. But the first servant refused.

Instead, he had his fellow servant thrown into prison until he could repay the debt. Seeing what happened, the other servants reported this to the king. Angry that the first servant hadn't shown the compassion he'd received, the king threw the unmerciful man into prison until he could repay his debt.

Before I became a Christian, it had never occurred to me to forgive Uncle Norman. After reading this parable, I became convicted that God wanted me to extend to Uncle Norman the same forgiveness extended to me. This was a desire born of gratitude and obedience to God. I wanted to be like the merciful king and not the unmerciful servant.

Perhaps the scripture on forgiveness that most influenced me was Luke 23:34, where Jesus cries out to God as he lay dying on the cross, *"Father, forgive them, for they know not what they do."*

That Jesus could say this while in such horrific pain of the very people who'd caused his crucifixion was incomprehensible to me. But if Jesus could do that, I knew I should be willing to forgive my uncle. Forgiving him would not diminish the terrible acts he'd committed, but it would release me from the intense hatred I carried towards him and my desire for revenge.

Contacting Uncle Ron for Uncle Norman's phone number, I finally mustered the courage to call. My heartbeat accelerated when I heard a male voice on the line.

"It's your niece, Mary," I said simply. It sounded so strange to speak those words. The last time we'd spoken was before walking into the police station together fourteen years earlier.

"Well, hello there," my uncle's voice responded nervously.

"I called to tell you I forgive you for what you did."

"Did you become a nun or something?" He sounded quite serious.

"No. I've recently become a Christian."

"Oh."

I'm sure my phone call and comments took him by surprise. The rest of the conversation lasted less than a minute before I said goodbye.

As we spoke, it didn't occur to me to ask why he'd tried to murder me or to get a first-hand account of what made him stop. Deep down, I wanted him to apologize, so I was surprised and disappointed that he sounded as though he didn't care one way or the other. Since I believed that one day he would go to hell for what he'd done, it didn't occur to me either to tell him God could forgive him for his past as God had forgiven me. My only goal that day was to forgive him.

And in spite of his reaction, I was proud of what God had enabled me to do. My forgiveness was completely sincere. After the call, I felt free from the hate I'd carried towards my uncle and the desire for revenge. It was another part of my emotional healing.

With all this, it still didn't cross my mind to report Uncle Norman to the police. I suppose I assumed that after so many years it was too late to press charges.

Around this time, Uncle Ron called to tell me my father was living in Mississippi and recovering from a heart attack. He gave me my father's phone number in case I wanted to call him. "I'm sure he'd like to hear from you."

Almost seven years had passed since I'd last heard from my father. I assumed he'd asked Uncle Ron to call me instead of contacting me directly because he felt some shame and hesitation over his frequent disappearing acts. But despite his past behavior, I wanted a relationship with my father and called him right away.

When he answered the phone, he sounded in good shape. To avoid conflict, I didn't ask why he'd left, and he didn't say. In truth, he seemed such a complex character that I couldn't understand his behavior. Whatever the reason, I chose to forgive him and welcome him back into my life. I hoped it was for good this time.

My family still didn't know the truth about Uncle Norman. I wanted to tell them, but only when the time was right. One evening when I was visiting my mom, she was unusually quiet.

"What's the matter?" I asked.

"I was laid off weeks ago," Mom said. "I hadn't told anyone because I didn't want you girls to be concerned. And I thought I could find another job right away. But now I don't know how I'm going to pay my bills."

"Do you want to move in with me?" I offered. "We could get a two-bedroom apartment."

"No, I don't want you to give up your beautiful apartment. You'll never find another one with a garage and fireplace for that price. Besides, this is the first time in my life I've lived alone, and I like it."

"Well, don't worry," I said. "Chrissy and I will take care of your bills until you find something else."

Chrissy and I paid Mom's bills while she looked for another job. I didn't tell anyone that to handle the additional bills I was eating peanut butter and jelly sandwiches every day for lunch and bagels with cream cheese or peanut butter most nights for dinner. My checking account zeroed out each payday.

Every week I brought groceries to Mom. We spent a lot of time together and became extremely close. We spoke on the phone daily. That was more important to me than what I ate. We often talked about my new Christian faith and all I was learning about God and Jesus.

"I was taught about Jesus as a little girl when I first went to the orphanage," Mom told me, "and I've prayed to him ever since."

"Have you ever read the Bible?" I asked.

"No, it's too hard to understand."

"They have a lot of versions out now that are easier to read. I'll buy you one."

I bought Mom an easy-to-read Bible, and three months later she rededicated her life to God. She hadn't been to church in years, but she began attending my church with me and underwent adult baptism. She found a job as a private caretaker for the elderly. God gradually healed her of her pain and grief over Ed's death and enabled her to forgive my father for disappearing and not paying child support.

This transformed attitude also gave Mom new compassion for my father. She'd come to believe he suffered from post-traumatic stress disorder due to his World War II service in the South Pacific, where he'd witnessed the gruesome deaths of friends and narrowly escaped death himself, including a severe bout of dengue fever. She reiterated stories of his tragic childhood filled with neglect and abuse.

"Your father never dealt with his issues," she told me. "I think the combination of his difficult childhood and war experiences contributed to his inability to care for his family. His life might have turned out differently if he'd received counseling."

Perhaps his dysfunctional childhood was the reason he acted the way he did as an adult, though that was still no excuse.

Eventually, I knew it was time to tell Mom the truth about Uncle Norman. It was a topic we'd avoided for years because it was too painful. But now that God had freed me from hatred towards Uncle Norman, I wanted her to experience that freedom as well. I also wanted her to know the truth.

Confident she was now strong enough to hear the details, I called her. "Are you going to be home tomorrow night?"

"Yes, why?"

"I just wanted to stop by after work. I'll see you then."

CHAPTER TWENTY-ONE

The Vision

If the son therefore shall make you free, ye shall be free indeed.

—John 8:36

I prayed all the way to Mom's house the next evening, dreading our upcoming conversation. I could only imagine what it would be like for any parent to hear the particulars of such a gruesome assault on their beloved child. "Dear heavenly Father, please give me the right words to say!"

When I arrived, we gave each other a big hug. Then Mom made herself comfortable in her rocking chair while I knelt on the floor next to her. "Mom, there's something I need to talk to you about."

Mom straightened up anxiously. "What's wrong?"

"Nothing is wrong. There's just something I've been wanting to tell you."

First, I explained how I'd called Uncle Norman to tell him I forgave him and how this had freed me from the hatred I carried towards him. Then I told her how Uncle Norman had sexually abused me for three years prior to the assault.

Horrified, Mom burst into tears. Getting up, I grabbed a box of tissues and handed them to Mom. But I couldn't stop there. I waited for her to recover her composure, patting her and speaking to her soothingly. Only then did I tell her the full story of that horrible night. She became hysterical as I related the gory details of what I'd endured. I wrapped my arms around her to comfort her.

"Mom, all these years I've had a 'why me' attitude because of what I went through and never once thought how miraculous it was that I'd survived. I've now come to realize that God saved my life that day. He also spared you from the pain you would have gone through if I was murdered."

"I wouldn't have survived if he killed you," she cried.

"I know." I could no longer hold back my own tears as I explained to Mom the transformation in my heart and how God was healing me from all Uncle Norman had done to me. "Mom, I never told you this, but for years I wished I was never born because of what happened. God has changed all that. I feel like a different person. Now I feel so blessed that I survived. I believe it was a true miracle."

Once Mom could control her tears, she began telling me about her own experience that Valentine's Eve. "I was very worried that your uncle had you out so late. When you still weren't home by your bedtime, I knew something must be wrong. I grabbed my rosaries and got on my knees to pray. A little after midnight, your Uncle Norman called to say his car had broken down. I told him to get you home right away or I was calling the police."

I didn't remember Mom ever telling me Uncle Norman had called her. She may have told me that night or the next day, but if she did, I'd completely forgotten about it. I smiled as I realized something I'd never understood.

"So when he looked for a phone booth that night, it was to call you with the lie that his car had broken down. You probably scared him half to death when you yelled at him. I always wondered why he decided to turn himself in. He may have thought he was safer with the police than with you. He probably thought you'd kill him when you saw the condition I was in."

Mom managed a chuckle. "Yes, I probably would have."

The momentary humor lightened the atmosphere fractionally, giving us a much-needed respite from the intensity of our conversation.

"So what happened next?" I asked.

"Well, it was maybe between one and two in the morning when the police called and asked me to meet them at the hospital. I ran next door and asked Phyllis to drive me. I put Chrissy in charge of Ed and left."

"Yes, I remember you showing up at the hospital in your pajamas."

"Months later, I found out your uncle was living with my friend Barbara," Mom continued. "You remember her, don't you?"

"Of course."

"We got into an argument over it, but the next day Barbara called to say she'd told Norman to leave. She didn't want to lose our friendship over him. While he was moving out, he told Barbara that St. Anthony had appeared to him while he was assaulting you, and that's what made him stop."

I vaguely remembered the St. Anthony ring Uncle Norman had always worn on his right ring finger. While my uncle rarely attended church, I'd heard him mention more than once in my childhood how St. Anthony was his own particular patron saint.

Of course, I didn't believe for a minute that St. Anthony or any human being now in heaven had appeared to my uncle. But I did believe God had sent an angel my uncle assumed to be his patron saint to stop him. It all made sense now why he'd dropped the hatchet and sat there staring and crying in such a strange way, giving me time to grab the hatchet and throw it out of the car. And his vision must have been what finally impelled him to turn himself in.

"So God truly did perform a miracle to save me!" I exclaimed. We were both emotionally drained by the time I left but also in awe of how God had miraculously spared my life.

The following evening, I went to see Chrissy. She was stunned and in tears as I shared the full details of that horrible evening. Then she shared her own memory of that evening. When I still wasn't home by our usual bedtime on school nights, she'd felt something bad was happening to me. It wasn't just the normal worry because Uncle Norman still hadn't brought me home at such a late hour. She'd had such a strong inner conviction I was in danger that she'd eventually gotten out of bed to tell Mom. She'd found Mom sitting in her rocker in front of the TV, but instead of watching the show she was praying out loud, her rosary beads in her hands. When the police called and Mom rushed off, Chrissy had known she was right that something terrible had happened.

We also discussed Uncle Norman's vision of St. Anthony. Chrissy remembered Mom telling her that story. Then her expression turned sad and troubled. "You know, I always blamed myself for what Uncle Norman did to you."

I stared at my twin with astonishment. "Why in the world would you blame yourself? You didn't have anything to do with it."

She gave an unhappy sigh. "There's a secret I never told anyone. The week before Uncle Norman tried to murder you, he asked me to go shopping with him. About twenty minutes into the ride, I realized he wasn't driving in the right direction for the store. I felt something was wrong like an inner voice warning me of danger. I told him he'd better turn the car around or I was jumping out. He did, but not before making me promise I wouldn't tell Mom. I kept my promise, but I heard that same inner voice the next week when I felt something bad was happening to you."

I was glad Chrissy had finally shared with me the burden she'd kept for so many years. Quickly, I reassured her, "It wasn't your fault. Even if you'd told Mom, she wouldn't have suspected what he was planning. No one could have imagined it. Besides, he'd only have lied and said he got lost or took a wrong turn."

I took a deep breath before adding, "There's more I've never told. Uncle Norman started sexually abusing me when I was about nine."

Chrissy shot up straight, her eyes widening in shock. "Really! He abused me too."

"What?" I was just as stunned by her secret. Comparing notes, we quickly discovered that Uncle Norman had threatened both of us to never tell.

By now we were both in tears. Grabbing a handful of tissues, Chrissy handed me a wad. Wiping at my tears, I could feel my anger against Uncle Norman surging up again. "Chrissy, I'm so sorry!"

My heart ached for my twin. Now that I knew she'd also experienced sexual abuse, I shared how Jesus was freeing me from the pain of my past and how he could heal her too. I prayed with her before I left. But for the next few weeks I struggled to control my renewed anger towards Uncle Norman. It was easier to forgive him for what he'd done to me than what he'd done to someone I cared about.

It took weeks to work through my emotions, but at last I was able to get rid of the latest bout of anger towards my uncle. For the first time in my life, I felt truly free from the dark clouds and evil force that had tormented me from my youth. By now I had learned that this evil force is actually the devil, whom I'd believed to be a myth until I became a Christian. The Bible is full of scriptures that taught me the reality of Satan as an actual being who hates people and delights in controlling, tormenting, and destroying them. One such scripture is 1 Peter 5:8:

> Be sober, be vigilant; because your adversary the devil, as a roaring lion, walketh about, seeking whom he may devour.

While I no longer doubted Satan's existence, he also no longer controlled my life. Even when I couldn't always feel the invisible presence of God's Holy Spirit, I took comfort from God's promise in Hebrews 13:5:

> Never will I leave you, never will I forsake you.

God was always with me, but now that I was maturing as a Christian, he wanted me to believe it based on faith rather than feelings.

Chapter Twenty-Two

The List

Knowing this, that the trying of your faith worketh patience.

—James 1:3

O ne of my new Christian friends, Louise, was all aglow as we discussed her upcoming wedding at work one day.

"I mailed in my RSVP," I told her. "I'll be going by myself. I wish I could meet the right person to share my life with, but I don't know if it will ever happen. I've always admired couples who have celebrated fifty years together."

"I didn't think it would happen to me either," Louise responded. "I mean, here I am, divorced with five kids. My heart's desire was to find a sensitive Christian man with a sense of humor who would love me and my children. I asked God to either fulfill that desire or change my heart. Then when I was in Israel last year, I wrote out my prayer request and put it into the Wailing

Wall. Three months later, I met my fiancé. He's everything I asked God for in a mate."

I was amazed. I'd never thought to ask God for a mate, let alone be so specific. Louise quoted Psalm 37:4:

> Delight thyself also in the LORD: and he shall give thee
> the desires of thine heart.

"If your desire is to be married," she added, "I recommend you make a list of the qualities you want in a husband and submit that list to God in prayer. God will either fulfill that desire or change your heart."

I hadn't been on a date since I'd become a Christian. Now her words gave me a glimmer of hope. "Thanks. I'll work on it tonight."

That evening I got out my Bible and read through Psalm 37:4 several times. Then I picked up a pen and found a notepad to make a list of the qualities I wanted in a mate. Pen in hand, I hesitated. *I better pray first. I don't want to ask for a mate with the wrong characteristics.*

"Dear heavenly Father, please guide me as to the qualities I need to look for in a husband. In Jesus's name, amen."

I stared at the blank notepad in deep thought. Finally, my thoughts—and the ink—began flowing.

Is a Christian or will be someday. As a fairly young Christian, I didn't consider it crucial that my future mate needed to be one when we met, but it was definitely crucial he become one at some point.

Older than me. I was usually attracted to older men, though I'd dated a few my age. At almost twenty-seven, I hoped to meet someone in his thirties.

Taller than me. He didn't have to be tall, just taller. To a lot of women this might not be a big deal, but to me it was important. At five feet, five-and-a-half inches, I was neither short nor unusually tall for a woman. But I'd been tall for my age in my pre-teen years and still felt like a big girl. I wanted someone taller so I could feel smaller.

Sense of humor. I was very much attracted to a man who could make me laugh. I wouldn't be opposed to one who was serious, but he also needed to possess a sense of humor.

Weight conscious. Ever since joining Weight Watchers, I'd exercised, ate healthier, and managed to keep off those extra ten pounds. I wanted someone who cared about his appearance as well.

Financially stable. This was very important. I didn't want to struggle financially as we'd done throughout my childhood.

Would be my best friend. I not only wanted to share my life with someone, but wanted him to be my best friend.

Saying a prayer, I tucked the list inside my wallet with excitement and anticipation. Since it had only taken Louise three months to meet her future husband, I expected God to send my mate soon. While waiting, I spent a lot of time with family, including Hazel, who was still involved in our lives and like a grandmother to us until she passed away some time later at the age of eighty-one.

Chrissy was into jogging and ran in local races, including the annual Thanksgiving Turkey Trot five-kilometer race. Three days before the race, she convinced me to register even though I'd never even jogged. I came in last place but was proud of myself for finishing. After that, I jogged three to five times a week to stay in shape.

In addition to my female friends, I became good friends with a few single male Christians, though our relationships were strictly platonic. We hiked up mountains, went to movies, attended Christian concerts, and went out to dinner. It was nice to have some normal male companionship, but I still longed for that special someone.

Three years after I became a Christian, Chrissy called to tell me she'd experienced a spiritual awakening. She told me how she'd gone from being angry at me after I became a Christian to being scared I might be caught in some cult to being curious to eventually realizing that what I believed was real.

"One day I was praying about you and recounting all of my good deeds. I felt God telling me those deeds were as filthy rags because I was trying to earn my salvation through works and that I was no better than you'd been before you became a Christian. I knew right then I needed to repent of my self-righteousness."

Chrissy prayed to accept Jesus as her Savior, asked him to forgive her of her sins, committed her life to him, and began attending a nearby church with excellent Bible teaching.

Meanwhile, I was growing discouraged about my future mate. Two years went by, during which time I went on only two dates.

Both consisted of going to the movies, and the relationships didn't go beyond the first date. From time to time, I pulled out my list and prayed. I couldn't understand why I hadn't met anyone when Louise had met the man she would marry only three months after she prayed.

Though it was difficult at times, God used this period to do a lot of work in me. The more I read the Bible, the more I changed. I no longer felt ugly, dirty, or had low self-esteem. I no longer felt different because of what Uncle Norman had done to me. I was now ready for a wholesome, normal relationship.

One day while reading the Bible, I came across Genesis 2:18:

> And the Lord God said, "It is not good that the man should be alone; I will make him an help meet for him."

It wasn't the first time I'd read that scripture. But this time it felt as though God was telling me directly that he had someone specifically for me. Comforted, I held on to that promise. It was one of many times I sensed God speaking to me as I read the Bible.

That same year, I was watching *The 700 Club* when an inner voice told me that one day I would share my own story of dramatic transformation on their program and that I would write a book. Those were things I would never have thought on my own, and I knew that inner voice came from God.

I still worked for Patrick Enunzio and even received two more promotions. When co-workers asked about my social life, I would tell them about my prayer list for a mate with certain qualities.

"That's ridiculous," one male co-worker responded derisively. "You need to go to the nightclubs or join a singles club."

"I'm not interested in that lifestyle anymore," I told him firmly. "Nor am I interested in any singles clubs."

"What do you think God's going to do?" he jeered. "Just drop him in your lap?"

"I don't know, but I know he's going to do it."

CHAPTER TWENTY-THREE

I'm Not Picky

He shall fulfill the desire of them that fear him.

—Psalm 145:19(a)

One day a co-worker named Jeff stopped by to see my boss. Patrick was on the phone, so while waiting, Jeff and I struck up a conversation.

"I'm surprised you haven't met someone yet," Jeff commented. "You're smart and attractive. Maybe you're just too picky."

"I'm not picky," I retorted. "I could date if I wanted, but I can't bring myself to go out with just anyone."

"Well, I can give you some advice on how to catch a man." He sounded quite serious.

"And what is that?"

"Men love it when women wear dresses. Also, most men are color blind. The only color they notice is red. I think you should buy some dresses, especially something in red. I bet you'll catch a man that way."

"If that's what it takes, I'll give it a try."

We both laughed, but I wondered if Jeff might be right. At a hundred and twenty-five pounds, I was the slimmest I'd been since my pre-teen years, thanks to the jogging regimen and healthy diet. I always looked very stylish and owned lots of beautiful clothes. But for years I'd mainly worn dress pants and blouses to work.

Deciding to take Jeff's advice, I went shopping during Macy's monthly One Day Sale. Clothes shopping had been one of my favorite activities since I was a teenager, and I still never paid full price. I bought a couple of dresses, one of which was red. I also couldn't resist a beautiful pair of red pants, a red chiffon blouse, and a red pair of shoes. The red pants outfit was very striking with my long, dark wavy hair, and I received compliments whenever I wore it.

I happened to be wearing my all-red outfit one day when I took Mom to the store to buy some house plants. After a while, I noticed a handsome man in his mid-thirties dressed in a long-sleeved shirt and tie staring at me. A few minutes later, he walked up and introduced himself as Stuart.

After some small talk about plants, Stuart asked if he could take me to dinner sometime. I was hesitant but ended up giving him my work number. He gave me a business card that indicated he was a stockbroker. After he left, Mom and I talked about my encounter with this seemingly charming young man.

"He seems nice, Mom. I don't think his intentions can be bad since he approached me while I was with you. Who knows, maybe he's the one."

He did appear to meet the outward qualifications on my list—taller, older, nice appearance, good job—so I decided to give him a chance. The next day he called and asked to take me to dinner the following Saturday night. Out of caution, I suggested we meet at the restaurant.

When the night of our dinner date finally arrived, I couldn't decide what to wear. It was my first date in over a year. I changed outfits five times, and my bedroom looked like a bomb had hit it by the time I settled on an all-white summer outfit.

I arrived at the restaurant early. Stuart walked in a few minutes later, looking just as handsome as I remembered. Throughout the entire meal, he seemed a little on the anxious side as though in a hurry. But when we finished, he asked, "Would you like to go someplace else for dessert?"

"Sure!" I wasn't ready for our date to end, and I was glad to know he felt the same way.

"There's a nice little bistro in that shopping center just up the street," he suggested.

"I know which one you mean. I'll follow you in my car," I said, still being cautious.

I found it adventurous to follow at Stuart's bumper as our two vehicles pulled out onto the street. We soon reached the shopping center Stuart had mentioned, which had several nice restaurants and bistros on the premises. But Stuart just kept driving on down the street. We'd gone another quarter-mile when he suddenly pulled into a hotel parking lot.

Pulling in next to his car, I rolled down the window. As he climbed out of the driver's seat, I asked, "Why are we here? The bistro you mentioned was back there in the shopping center."

Instead of answering, he looked in the direction of the hotel. "Have you been here before?"

"No," I responded sharply. *Why in the world is he asking me this when we're supposed to be going to a bistro for dessert?*

"You're sure you haven't been here?"

"I'm positive," I said, now with considerable agitation. "Why are we here?"

That was when I suddenly realized the dessert he wanted to have was me!

"You're such a jerk!" I spat out at him angrily. Rolling up my window, I sped off. I was near tears the entire drive home, but I was too angry to cry. *What a jerk, jerk, jerk! Ugh!*

I was especially upset with myself for having been so naïve. As soon as I got home, I called Mom and told her about my disastrous date. As always, she was a great consolation.

On Monday morning, Stuart called me at work to apologize. "I'd like another chance," he begged.

"I'm not interested," I told him and hung up without giving him the opportunity to say another word. My co-worker's suggestion to wear red sure hadn't worked out the way I wanted, but that red outfit did give me an evening I never forgot!

When I got home from work, I tore up my prayer list for a mate. Several days later, I regretted it. I didn't need that piece of paper for God to answer my prayers, but I wanted it as a reminder. I ran downstairs to pull my trash out of the barrel only to discover it had already been picked up.

Disappointed, I chose not to rewrite my list. Whenever I got discouraged, I reminded myself of God's promises in Genesis 2:18 and Psalm 37:4. But it was an ongoing battle.

I'd told one of my friends about my disastrous date with Stuart. A week later she called me. "I arranged a lunch date for you with a Christian friend of my cousin. He sounds like he fits the requirements on your list."

"Sorry, but I'm not interested," I insisted. "I don't go on blind dates."

"It's too late. He's already expecting to meet you tomorrow. His name is Victor Baron."

I continued to protest, but somehow she convinced me to meet Victor for lunch. Thirty-six years old, he was easy on the eyes and looked as if he played professional football. He worked in the pharmaceutical industry and seemed quite charismatic. I didn't hesitate when he asked to take me to dinner the following Saturday. I felt comfortable enough to give him my home phone number and address.

Victor called to tell me he'd made reservations at a very elegant historic restaurant about an hour away. He picked me up in his brand-new Lincoln, and I settled in, looking forward to the long scenic drive. My excitement ended when Victor inserted a children's musical cassette into his tape player. I'd been a big fan of such music as a child and even enjoyed some as an adult. But it just felt weird to me that a thirty-six-year-old man would play children's music on his first date with a grown woman.

I didn't make any comments about it, but I was uncomfortable and already couldn't wait for the date to end. Victor was very engaging throughout our meal and return ride home, but my mind was elsewhere. As soon as he'd walked me to my door and said goodnight, I called my friend and told her what happened.

"You're just being silly," she said. "I'm sure it was perfectly innocent."

I decided to ask one of my male friends about it. But he didn't see things as I did.

"It doesn't sound abnormal to me. Some of that music is quite popular with adult males and females. It can be quite catchy and upbeat."

It still didn't feel right to me. I would have preferred classical, smooth jazz, or contemporary Christian music. But later on I felt badly for thinking Victor was strange. He seemed like a genuinely good guy, and maybe he was just a big kid at heart. After all, the Bible does talk about Christians becoming like children in Matthew 18:3:

> Verily I say unto you, except ye be converted, and become as little children, ye shall not enter into the kingdom of heaven.

Victor must have sensed my urgency for the date to end because I didn't hear from him again. As always, I called Mom and told her about my date.

"No more blind dates for me," I told her. "I'm waiting for God to bring my future husband into my life naturally. I don't want to force it."

CHAPTER TWENTY-FOUR

The Return

If it be possible, as much as lieth in you, live peaceably with all men.

—Romans 12:18

A fter that initial phone call, I had remained in touch with my father. Every time he called, he would check up on the status of my love life. I filled him in on my latest dates and other social activities. But now I could only report that I wasn't dating at all.

"I could date if I wanted to," I made clear. "I get asked out occasionally, just not by anyone I'm interested in. I don't want to go out with just anyone. I want to be with the right one."

"It'll happen one of these days," he would encourage me. "The perfect guy for you is out there somewhere."

When I was thirty, my father moved back to New York with his girlfriend Sylvia, which enabled Chrissy and me to visit him on a regular basis. An attractive woman ten years younger than my father, Sylvia had the light-blonde hair, lithe height, and svelte body of a stereotypical California beach girl. But in personality she was quiet-spoken and even-tempered, a contrast to my stubborn, quick-tempered father.

Since our schedules were so different, Chrissy and I typically visited my father separately except for holidays. I would spend a Saturday just hanging out with him and Sylvia. Sometimes I stayed overnight. Each time I had to leave, my father would get teary-eyed.

One topic my father and I never discussed was Uncle Norman. It was as if he didn't exist. Nor was I ready to tell my father the truth about what his brother had done to me. But I did learn a lot more about where my father had been since moving out of Uncle Ron's house more than two decades earlier. As he'd vowed to Mom so many times, he'd headed straight to California, where he'd lived under the assumed name of Cary Haskell.

"Why that name?" I asked. Cary was, of course, my father's and paternal grandfather's first name, but I'd never heard of any Haskells.

"That was the last name of the couple who lived next door to me when I was a kid. The ones who fed me on occasion and the wife paid me to carry her groceries."

My father had met Sylvia sometime after he'd moved to California. He'd also started his own business of moving and restoring furniture. After years of job instability, my father had finally found a profitable livelihood that he liked. Maybe if he'd found that niche a few years earlier, my parents might still be together. Or maybe not!

My father hadn't stayed in California for long. He'd continued moving from state to state every couple of years, taking his furniture business wherever he went. His explanation for moving so often and living under an alias was fear that Mom might find him and have him arrested for not paying child support.

He also had a very different viewpoint on his disappearance from our lives when I was six. In his thinking, Mom was to blame for having gone on welfare and not taking him back after his escapade with the waitress. That his own bad behavior and inability to provide for us might have contributed was not something he would even consider.

"Your mother took you kids away from me," he would tell me indignantly.

"No she didn't," I responded. "You could have continued to visit us whenever you wanted. She never stopped you from seeing us."

His face grew red with anger, as it always did when I defended Mom, so I quickly changed the subject. I could have asked why he'd disappeared a second time when I was eighteen since he could hardly blame that on Mom. But as someone who avoided conflict at all cost, I chose to drop the topic.

My father had continued with follow-up appointments over his heart condition at the VA hospital in New York. A year after his return, he called me. "My doctor is scheduling an artificial valve replacement for me at the VA hospital in Boston. I'll be there for a month."

"Is Sylvia going with you?" I asked.

"No, I need her to stay here to take care of the business. I'll be okay."

I felt badly that he was facing major surgery with no family for moral support. I knew Chrissy couldn't leave her job and husband that long, so I did some research, then called my father back. "I'm going to Boston with you. I have more than enough unused paid vacation, and I found a room to rent just a block from the hospital."

"That would be nice." Though my father's words were nonchalant, I could hear very real emotion in his voice over my offer.

During that month in Boston, I spent as much time with my father as hospital regulations allowed. Whenever he fell sleep, I would visit other heart patients to encourage and pray with them. I also kept in close contact with Sylvia, Mom, and Chrissy to keep them informed of his condition.

The operation was a success, and he returned home with a new heart valve that ticked so loud I could hear it when I put my ear to his chest. Those weeks with my father helped heal the loss from his earlier absence from my life.

Once my father made a full recovery, he called to tell me he wanted to buy a piece of land near where he and Sylvia were living and put a trailer on it. I was surprised since the last time he'd owned property was when my parents bought their bungalow shortly after their wedding. But I liked the idea of my father putting down roots and not running off again, so I responded enthusiastically. "That's great! Do you already have a property in mind?"

He cleared his throat, and I suddenly realized where this conversation was headed. "Well, actually, I need five thousand dollars and was wondering if you could lend me the money. I'll pay you back five hundred dollars a month."

I'm not sure how my father knew I had a savings account, but it was the first time I'd had one since graduating from Katharine Gibbs. Maybe he assumed I had extra cash because of the month I took off from work to spend with him in Boston. Either way, I wanted my father to remain close by, so I agreed to the loan. When I went to visit him, he showed me the property. It was secluded, which seemed a perfect fit since my father didn't socialize other than Sylvia, a few family members, and when necessary with his customers. In the end, my father did miss an occasional payment, but he had the entire loan paid off in just over a year.

By this point, I'd decided it was time to tell my father the truth about Uncle Norman. Especially since I'd become aware that he had allowed Uncle Norman to actually live with him off and on. Since that day my uncle had turned himself in to the police, he'd never held another steady job and had spiraled further and further into alcoholism. While my father didn't know all his brother had done to Chrissy and me, he certainly knew about the beating and arrest, so it troubled and confused me that my father would give shelter to his daughter's assailant. It was time he understood the full extent of what his brother had done to me.

I made plans to visit the following Saturday so I could tell my story in person. After lunch, we sat at the kitchen table while my father told me stories from his past. These included some youthful escapades with Uncle Ron when the two of them were trying to make a fast buck.

One such incident involved an attempt to steal a safe. My father was outside on lookout while Uncle Ron was inside trying to push the safe out a window. Suddenly my father heard the wailing of police sirens. He took off with lightning speed, leaving Uncle Ron behind. The next day my father bailed Uncle Ron out of jail, who gave him a furious earful for having left his younger brother behind to be arrested.

As far as I know, my father was never arrested for stealing. But he did tell me of getting arrested while stationed in the Pacific during WWII. My father had been sent to deliver important documents to his commanding officer. He was driving along in a jeep when he encountered a young woman. Instead of delivering the papers, he went AWOL with the young woman for two full days. When his commanding officer found out, my father was arrested and spent the next three months in the stockade, as the army "jail" was called. He would likely have been court-martialed, but when the commanding officer was transferred elsewhere, one of his buddies faked a wire communication that commuted my father's sentence to time served. He was released a short time later, completed his time in the service, and was honorably discharged.

When he told me that story, I wondered if the trauma of being thrown in the stockade was what made my father so fearful of being arrested over child support. I waited until Sylvia joined us before bringing up the reason for my visit. "I need to tell you both something."

By the time I'd finished telling them what Uncle Norman had done to me and Chrissy, my father's eyes were filled with tears. Sylvia too was in shock, since she'd known Uncle Norman for almost fifteen years and, like my father, saw him as a sweet, harmless, frail old man who needed their help.

My father cleared his throat before admitting, "I didn't hear that Norman had beat you up until Ron told me years later. Norman was living with us at the time. When I found out what he'd done, I grabbed my gun and chased him out of the house, threatening to shoot him."

Would my father have actually shot his brother if he'd known the full extent of Uncle Norman's attempts to kill me? For that matter, was my father's story even true? It seemed unlikely it had taken years to find out about Uncle Norman's arrest and confession when the entire family had been looking for him to let him know. And if Uncle Norman could find him so easily, why had Uncle Ron and their other siblings insisted they had no idea where he'd disappeared? And once he did find out, why had my father continued to take Uncle Norman in over the years?

None of it really made sense to me. But then when had my father's actions or Uncle Norman's ever made sense to me? Whatever the full story, I was relieved as I left their house that I'd finally told my father and Sylvia the truth.

A year later, I was on the phone with my father when he informed me that Uncle Norman had once again moved in with him and Sylvia. I was stunned and felt deeply betrayed as though my father had chosen Uncle Norman over Chrissy and me. The last time I'd seen Uncle Norman was at the police station twenty years earlier. Yes, I'd forgiven him and was no longer afraid of my uncle. But I certainly didn't want to see him face-to-face, much less in my own father's home. How could my father even consider such a thing now that he knew the whole truth?

I asked God for guidance before responding firmly, "You realize I can't visit you at home while Uncle Norman is living with you."

"I understand. But I feel sorry for him." My father went on to make excuses for his brother as though Uncle Norman was some helpless child. "He's a pathetic alcoholic who lives with anyone he can find who will provide odd jobs for him to earn his keep. He doesn't have anywhere else to go right now, and I could really use his help with our business."

Despite my sense of betrayal, I didn't want to cut off contact with my father. "Fine, but if you want to see me, we'll have to meet at a restaurant."

"That's fine," my father agreed.

The following week, Chrissy called to tell me she'd gone unannounced to our father's house to confront Uncle Norman. When she got out of her car, she saw him in the garage refinishing a piece of furniture.

"Oh, hi. Which one are you?" he asked.

"I'm the one you didn't try to kill," Chrissy responded.

At that moment, our father burst into the garage, yelling at Chrissy, "Don't do anything!"

Chrissy stood her ground, demanding, "How can you have this man living with you?"

"It's complicated," our father told her. "Just go inside."

While Uncle Norman stayed in the garage, our father asked Chrissy to take a ride with Sylvia to pick up some cooked chicken for dinner. On the way, Sylvia tried to explain to Chrissy that she didn't doubt my story but that a lot of bad things had happened to Uncle Norman when he was young. To Chrissy, it felt as though Sylvia, like my father, was making excuses for the person who had hurt her and her twin so deeply, and she was not about to accept those excuses.

Once Chrissy and Sylvia returned to the house, Sylvia set four place settings for dinner at the kitchen table. As Sylvia and my father sat down, Chrissy picked up one of the place settings and put it on top of a cabinet on the other side of the room.

"He's not eating at the table with us," she said with authority.

Uncle Norman ate on the other side of the room and was kept out of the dinner conversation. As soon as everyone finished eating, Chrissy said her goodbyes to our father and Sylvia.

Heading out the door, she turned to give Uncle Norman one final disgusted glare.

Staring back at her, he said pleadingly, "Pray for me."

Those words pierced right through her. How was she supposed to deal with such a request? Chrissy didn't call my father for at least a month after that visit. Occasionally, I got together with him at a diner not far from his home, but we never mentioned Uncle Norman. We tried to act like things were normal, but our visits were strained.

Then about nine months after Uncle Norman moved in, he moved out. Visits to my father's home returned to normal. Once again, no one mentioned Uncle Norman.

CHAPTER TWENTY-FIVE

Revelations

He revealeth the deep and secret things.

—Daniel 2:22(a)

T wo years later, Mr. Right had still not walked into my life. At thirty-three, I was growing increasingly disgusted with my smoking habit. I felt God didn't want me to be addicted to anything, and I was definitely addicted to cigarettes.

I also knew it wasn't healthy. For one, it made jogging more difficult. Almost everyone I hung around with didn't smoke. They never condemned or criticized me, but I felt like an oddball every time I excused myself to smoke outside.

For the umpteenth time, I vowed to quit as soon as I'd smoked the last cigarette in my latest carton. I was out of cigarettes when I arrived at work the next morning. As I drank a cup of coffee, the urge to smoke hit me, but I resisted. The urge returned at lunch and dinner. Once again, I managed to resist.

But by late evening, I could resist no longer. I went out to buy a pack of cigarettes and began smoking. The next morning I was so frustrated with myself that I broke the remaining cigarettes into small pieces and threw them in the trash. I managed to last the day at work without smoking. But after dinner, I rummaged through my trash, picking out any piece of broken cigarette with enough tobacco to smoke.

The next morning I bought a pack on my way to work. That night, I flushed the remaining cigarettes down the toilet along with the remnants in the trash. I couldn't understand why I kept failing to break this unhealthy cycle when God's power was available to me.

I asked God why I couldn't beat my addiction. That small inner voice I'd learned to trust made clear to me that I wasn't really willing to give up cigarettes. I knew this to be true. Since I was nineteen, my Marlboros had been a crutch, calming me down during times of stress.

I realized I needed to change how I prayed about this issue. I'd been asking for deliverance. I needed to ask for willingness.

"Dear heavenly Father, please help me be willing to give up cigarettes," I began praying. "I know what this is doing to my body isn't honoring to you. And I know that I really don't want to give them up. But I do *want* to want to stop smoking. Only you can give me that willingness, so please change my desires. In Jesus's name, amen."

I asked for Friday off, so I would have three full days away from work. For the entire three days I prayed, drank lots of juice (which I'd been told would help detoxify my body from the nicotine), and did not smoke a single cigarette. By the end of the third day, I had with God's help finally broken free from a fourteen-year addiction, and I never went back.

But I still saw no answer in sight as far as my prayers for a mate. I was beginning to feel like an old maid. My hope of being a couple who would eventually celebrate fifty years of marriage was quickly fading. Even as I continued to pray regarding my future husband, I wondered about the reason for the delay. With so much work God had already done in me, surely I couldn't be the holdup! Maybe my future spouse, whoever he might be, just wasn't ready yet to settle down.

Then I began wondering if the delay was connected to the abuse I'd suffered as a child. I made an appointment to meet with my pastor's wife Roberta about my situation. Sitting in my car before heading into the church for our meeting, I took a moment to pray. "Dear heavenly Father, I feel there is a blockage to my prayers for a mate. If there is and it relates to me, please show Roberta so I can work on it. In Jesus's name, amen."

Greeting me with a hug, Roberta led the way into her private office. Her first action was to pray that God would guide us into all truth. Then I explained why I was there.

"I've been praying for a husband for seven years. I've only been on a few dates since then. I feel something is blocking the answer to my prayers. It might be related to a very traumatic experience I went through as a child. I was hoping you would have some insight."

For the first time, I told her how I was almost murdered as a child. Her expression never changed. When I finished, I expected her to be in a state of shock. But I was the one astonished by her response.

"I feel as though the Holy Spirit is telling me you've never really accepted what happened to you. You tell it as though it happened to someone else."

"Really?" Her statement took me off guard. Before I'd become a Christian, I'd known I was in denial. But since I'd been able to talk about my experiences for the past seven years, I'd believed that problem was resolved.

"I also feel that the Holy Spirit is telling me you never forgave yourself for not telling the truth about what happened."

That statement took me by surprise as well. Then I realized she was right. I blamed myself that Uncle Norman was never imprisoned. If I'd told the truth when I was twelve, he might have been imprisoned for years or even the rest of his life. I'd never cut myself any slack that I was only twelve at the time and in extreme fear for my life if I told.

"I think you should pray about this," Roberta urged me.

She prayed with me again before I left. Walking back to my car, I reflected on our conversation and was grateful for what God had revealed to her. I also felt completely overwhelmed. Just when I'd thought I was healed from my past, God was showing me something else I needed to work on. I felt like an onion with God peeling off layers one by one.

I have been able to talk about my experiences more freely. But maybe there's more to it than that. Whatever it takes, I'm going to do it!

When I arrived home, I dropped to my knees, weeping and praying. "Dear heavenly Father, thank you for revealing to Roberta issues from my past I still need to address. I now know I have to forgive myself for not telling the truth. I was just a child, so it was only natural I was too frightened to tell. Please help me to forgive myself. And if I haven't truly accepted what happened to me, please help me to do that as well."

Two weeks after my meeting with Roberta, I hit the snooze button on my alarm more times than usual and overslept. Not wanting to be late for work, I jumped in the shower, washed my hair, and threw on a white chiffon dress with large yellow polka dots. I applied my makeup as fast as I could but didn't have time to blow-dry my long, thick dark hair.

When I arrived at my desk, the door leading into my boss's office was open. A handsome man with short brown hair and glasses was seated inside at a small conference table. I checked Patrick's calendar to see who the visitor might be, but my boss's calendar was clear, so the visitor was certainly no appointment I'd scheduled for my boss.

Heading over to pour myself a cup of coffee, I noticed a clipboard near the coffee pot that held some business papers. I could see the name Wally at the top of the paperwork, but a large clip covered any last name.

Could that be the name of Patrick's visitor? He sure doesn't look like a Wally!

For some reason, I pictured someone named Wally as having a nerdy look about him. This man was far from nerdy looking. From my desk right outside Patrick's office, I could hear him conversing with my boss. His voice was deep and masculine like the voice of a radio disc jockey.

He sure doesn't sound like a Wally either!

About twenty minutes later, my boss and his visitor emerged from the office. Patrick paused at my desk to introduce me. "Mary, this is Wally, a CPA from northern Virginia, who will be doing an audit in our building over the next four months."

So I'd been right as to the owner of that clipboard! Rising to my feet, I reached over the desk for a handshake. "Nice to meet you, Wally."

Wally's grip as he shook my hand was firm. At this distance, I could see that he was about five inches taller than me and even more handsome up close with his olive complexion and chiseled facial features. Muscled biceps and a flat stomach demonstrated that he worked out regularly. In fact, he looked the perfect blend of an accountant and personal fitness trainer.

And here I am looking like a drowned rat with my wet hair!

"Mary, could you help Wally locate any files he needs for his audit?" Patrick asked once introductions were complete.

"No problem. I'll be happy to help." And indeed I didn't mind this new assignment at all. Before Wally left, he handed me a business card. As I took it, I noticed he wasn't wearing a wedding band.

The following Monday began a pattern for the next four months. Wally would fly in early Monday morning from northern Virginia, rent a car at the airport, then drive to our building to begin work. When he finished up on Friday, he would return the rental car to the airport and fly back home to northern Virginia. During the week, he booked accommodations at a local hotel.

That first week, Wally stopped by my desk several times to ask about various files. He always lingered to chat, and our conversations would soon shift from business to personal matters. His sense of humor never failed to make me laugh. I loved his deep, masculine voice and found out that he actually had worked as a radio disc jockey for a few years after graduating from college.

By the second week, I was beginning to think his frequent visits might be an excuse to see me rather than any urgent need of files. Maybe he was as attracted to me as I'd been to him from our first meeting.

The third week, Wally invited me out to lunch. On our way back to the office, we walked past a shop with a display of wedding gifts in the front window. The display included a wedding cake accompanied by a pair of ornate knives.

"So why do they have two knives when you only need one to cut the cake?" I mused aloud.

"One is to cut the cake," Wally responded only half-jokingly. "The other is to stab you in the back!"

His comment was a disappointment as it made abundantly clear his view of marriage was far less positive than my own.

Okay, so maybe he's attracted to me, I reminded myself sternly. *But he came here to do an audit, nothing more. When it's over, he'll be gone.*

That didn't keep me from being drawn to Wally. By our second lunch date, I'd learned more about him, including that he was nine years older than me and worked out regularly. And did I mention his great sense of humor?

Older than me? Physically fit? Sense of humor? As I chatted with Wally across the lunch we'd ordered, I suddenly realized those were qualities I'd listed for my ideal mate. In the next instant, I realized Wally was the answer to my prayers. There was absolutely no question in my mind. While I didn't hear an audible voice from God, I knew without a doubt this was the man I was going to marry. After seven years, God had practically dropped him in my lap, just as one of my male co-workers had derisively told me would never happen.

By now my heart was pounding rapidly and continued to do so for the remainder of our lunch. I never said a word to Wally about my revelation. If I had, he would have certainly bolted. He had no idea he was eating lunch with a woman who had prayed seven years for a husband and that God had just revealed he was the one. But that very night I called Mom and Chrissy to tell them I'd met the man I was going to marry.

After that revelation, I prayed for Wally on a regular basis. I prayed that one day he would become a Christian. I also prayed that God would give me opportunities to share my faith with him.

Each Monday morning when a new work week started, I looked forward anxiously to his arrival at my desk.

Wally and I continued to go out to lunch together two or three times a week and eventually graduated to dinners and the local musical theater. I learned that Wally was raised by both parents in a middle-class family. His father was a retired lieutenant colonel in the U.S. Army. Over the course of Wally's childhood and teen years, the family had lived in Japan, France, and various U.S. cities. While his father was stationed in France, they'd travelled all over Europe. He had a younger sister my age in California and another who lived in France.

Wally also told me he'd gone through a divorce nine years earlier. He'd smoked cigarettes in his youth but quit right after college and didn't feel he could ever date a smoker. I was thankful I'd quit just weeks before we met.

On several occasions I shared my faith with Wally. He too had been raised Catholic and had attended a Catholic high school after the family moved back to the U.S. from France. While he was no longer a practicing Catholic nor attended any church, he had no objections to my own Christian faith. For my part, our differences in where we were spiritually didn't affect our relationship negatively in any way.

I eventually introduced Wally to my mom when I brought him as my date to a wedding she was also attending. Afterward, she gave me her opinion. "He's adorable. I like him."

But the end of Wally's four-month assignment was quickly approaching. On his last day, I left work early and drove to the airport so I could see him off. As we sat waiting for his flight (this was back before security gates when friends and family could still accompany passengers to boarding areas), I wondered anxiously whether Wally would mention wanting to see me again. I didn't know how we could manage a long-distance relationship, but I wanted to at least give it a try.

But as we chatted, Wally never once brought up the topic. When his flight was called, he gave me a quick hug and said goodbye. He'd never been one for public displays of affection, so I wasn't expecting a kiss. But I'd expected *some* indication he wanted to continue seeing me. As he headed for the boarding gate without looking back, my spirits plummeted further.

I stayed at the airport to watch his airplane take off. As soon as it was out of view, I walked back to my car with tears in my eyes. I'd been so convinced this was the man I was called to marry. Was it possible I'd misheard God?

CHAPTER TWENTY-SIX

A Familiar Voice

Trust in the Lord with all thine heart.

—Proverbs 3:5(a)

I'm sure he'll call you," Mom encouraged when I poured out my heartbreak to her. "Give him some time. You have to be patient and trust the Lord."

Mom was right. No matter what happened, trusting God and God's perfect timing was an area I definitely needed to work on.

That next Monday I was back at my desk trying not to get discouraged when the phone rang. Picking up the receiver, I gave my usual response. "Good afternoon, Mr. Enunzio's office."

"Is Mr. Enunzio there?" The male voice on the line had a strong New York accent. It also sounded familiar. But though I usually recognized my boss's regular callers, I couldn't quite place this voice.

"He's not here right now. But he should back in about an hour." I reached for a pen to jot down the caller's name and number. "Would you like me to have him call you?"

The voice on the line suddenly shifted in tone. "Hey, this is Wally."

I had to laugh. Wally was very good at disguising his voice, something he'd picked up during his stint as a disc jockey. He'd often used one of his imitations when he called while working on the audit and had fooled me every time.

"I just wanted to let you know I'll be back in town next month," he added in his normal deep voice. "I'm doing another audit for your government agency, so I'll be in and out of your building again for a few more months."

"That's great!" I tried not to let my voice project too much excitement and relief. *Now I know I heard God correctly!*

As soon as Wally and I finished chatting, I dialed Mom. When I relayed what had just happened, she said, "See, I told you that you needed to trust the Lord."

Wally called me every week until he arrived back in town. Once he returned, we picked up right where we'd left off. As the relationship became more serious, he began staying in town some weekends so we could have more time together. We went sightseeing, toured museums, and spent time with my family and friends.

We dated for almost a year before I told Wally about Uncle Norman. I'd hesitated to tell him, but felt he should know. He was completely accepting and understanding. In fact, the only thing he didn't understand was my reluctance to tell him in the first place.

The second audit assignment was followed by a third. There was no longer any question as to staying in touch. Not long after, Wally asked me to marry him, and we began making plans for a spring wedding.

In all this time, I'd prayed many times for God to confirm whether Wally was the right man for me. Especially since he'd never expressed personal faith in Jesus, though he always supported my own faith and church attendance. Each time I prayed, I felt a peace that Wally was indeed God's choice for me. Neither of us was perfect, but we were perfect for each other. And I also had faith that somehow through me God in his perfect timing would lead Wally to become a Christian.

I thought back on the seven years I'd waited for my mate. So many times I'd become discouraged. I hadn't understood why it was taking so long. Now I understood. Throughout those years, God had been working behind the scenes. Wally needed to be ready to settle down. He also needed to start the new job that would bring him to my hometown.

God also knew I needed those years to heal from my childhood traumas and be ready for a healthy marriage relationship. My healing was a gradual one as God gently peeled away the layers. My smoking addiction might have been another reason for the delay, since Wally would likely never have dated me if I still smoked.

Once we were engaged, Wally decided to rent out the condo he owned in northern Virginia and buy a house. He suggested I fly down to go house hunting with him. I was more than happy to do so. The last time I'd lived in an actual house was as an infant. Since I was old enough to have memories, we'd always lived in apartment rentals.

The first house we looked at was in a quiet neighborhood with wide-spaced houses and almost no vehicular traffic. Front yards were landscaped with crepe myrtles, cherry blossoms, dogwoods, and azalea bushes. The house itself was two thousand square feet on a half-acre lot shaded by dozens of pine, maple, and oak trees. There were three bedrooms, hardwood floors, a beautiful brick fireplace, two full bathrooms, and a screened porch.

"It's so beautiful," I told Wally, overwhelmed at the thought of living in such a house. I felt rather like Cinderella.

"Well, we have a few more to see before making our decision," Wally reminded calmly.

By the time I flew home, we'd narrowed our decision to two houses. In the end, Wally bought the first house we'd looked at. I was ecstatic about my new home, but less so about leaving my family.

"I'm going to miss you something awful when I move away," I told Mom.

"I'm going to miss you too, but I'm so happy you finally found someone."

We promised to write, call, and visit each other at least several times a year. I also invited Mom to move down with us. She didn't want to leave her own community and circle of friends, but promised to take me up on my offer if a time came when she couldn't take care of herself. I vowed to hold her to that promise.

Meanwhile, Wally and I both decided we wanted a small wedding with just immediate family and close friends. Calling my father, I told him the news. "Will you come?"

I knew seeing Mom after almost thirty years would be an issue. Sure enough, he immediately made clear that he wouldn't attend since Mom would be there.

"But I want you at my wedding!" I urged. "Mom's not going to get into an argument with you if that's what you're worried about. Besides, you've talked to each other several times in the last few years, so I thought everything was okay."

No matter what I said, my father refused to change his mind. I didn't want to hold my wedding without him, and I certainly wasn't going to have him present without Mom. The only solution I could think of was to elope.

I called Mom about my dilemma. She was very understanding. "Whatever you decide is okay with me. I just want you to be happy."

After discussing the situation, Wally and I agreed we'd elope, but it would be pre-planned. We picked a wedding day, and I made arrangements to be married by a minister with no family in attendance. We decided to go to Colonial Williamsburg for our honeymoon, then fly to Los Angeles for a week to meet Wally's father, a widower, and his sister Susie.

The month before I was to be married, I arrived home from work and noticed my answering machine light blinking. I hit the button and heard a vaguely familiar masculine voice. "This is a voice from your past."

Is that who I think it is?

I didn't have caller ID so had no way to know who had left the mysterious message or even see the caller's phone number. But I was absolutely sure I recognized the voice. The last time I'd heard it was fourteen years ago. My mind conjured up the long blond hair, blue eyes, and bronzed tan that could have graced the cover of a romance novel.

And the painful memories of how he'd used and dumped me. How I'd kept running back to him desperate for the smallest crumbs of attention. *Chad? Why would he be calling me after all these years?*

The mysterious message puzzled me for days. Then one evening the following week, the phone rang again. I picked it up.

"Mary?"

The instant I heard my name, I knew I hadn't been mistaken. Here I was about to get married, and the devil was trying to tempt me with the one man from my past I'd never been able to refuse.

But this time it wasn't going to work. I was a Christian now, and I had God's Holy Spirit on my side. "Hi, Chad. I thought I recognized your voice on my answering machine."

"So how are you?"

"I'm doing great," I said. "I heard you got married."

"Yeah. I'm separated now." He chatted away for a few minutes, sounding like the same old Chad. He asked about my job, and I told him I still worked in the same office. He finally got to the point and asked if he could see me.

"I'm not interested," I said firmly. "I'm a Christian now, and I'm getting married next month."

It was the first time I'd ever turned him down, and it felt great. I was a different person from that desperate, wounded young woman he'd known all those years ago. I respected myself and my lifestyle now, and I was eager to tell him how becoming a Christian had transformed my life.

Despite turning him down, my conversation with Chad ended cordially. I had zero interest in seeing him again and made that clear. But a few days later, Chad showed up at my office. His hair was shorter, he was a little huskier, but he still looked great. He told me he just wanted to see me to say goodbye.

To me, it felt like the devil wasn't happy that I hadn't taken the bait when Chad called, so he'd sent Chad in person, thinking that would make me fall for Satan's schemes.

"Goodbye Chad," I said firmly. "You take care of yourself."

And that was the end of Chad's reappearance in my life.

The remaining weeks were filled with pre-wedding activities. My co-workers threw me a huge going-away party with Mom and Chrissy in attendance. My family threw me a wedding shower. I spent time packing up my belongings for the move to northern Virginia.

Finally, the big day arrived. Almost nine years after I'd made out that list of qualities for my ideal mate, Wally and I were married in private by a minister in a church just as we'd planned.

CHAPTER TWENTY-SEVEN

A Plan

Trust in him at all times; ye people, pour out your heart before him.

—Psalm 62:8(a)

When we arrived in California, Wally's sister Susie organized a wedding party for us at their father's home on the Palos Verdes Peninsula, attended by friends, neighbors, and more cousins than I could count. I liked his family right away. The entire week was a whirlwind of activity that included a drive to Palm Springs where Wally's father owned a condo, attending *The Tonight Show* with Jay Leno, touring Hollywood, and dining at great restaurants.

After we returned to northern Virginia, Wally flew out of town on business, and I arranged a job interview. Then I set out for a walk around our new neighborhood. Our front yard and the other lawns were bright with pink and white dogwoods, red azalea bushes, red tulips, and golden daffodils. At one house, an older woman was pulling her mail out of her mailbox.

"Are you new in the neighborhood?" she asked me.

"Yes, I recently married and moved in two houses away."

"I heard there was a new bride in the neighborhood." The older woman introduced herself as Eileen and invited me in for tea. As we chatted, I found out that she too was a Christian.

I began attending church with Eileen and her husband. I always invited Wally, and he occasionally took me up on the offer. Eileen and her husband often invited us over for dinner and always for my birthday. I also started a new job as an executive secretary.

Wally worked out of town most weekdays, so we only saw each other on weekends. When he was home, I always said the blessing before dinner. He didn't seem to mind. I also prayed with him for God's blessing and protection on his travel before he flew out of town on business. I tried to be a Christian example without pressuring him to attend church or become a Christian.

I gradually made other friends at work, church, and in my neighborhood. I stayed in touch with my family via letters and phone calls and bought Mom her first airplane ticket to visit us. For Christmas, Wally and I traveled to New York to be with my family. A few days later, Mom returned to Virginia with us to celebrate Christmas all over again.

Chrissy and I were still helping Mom financially, and now that I was married, I could afford to contribute even more. It gave me such pleasure to spoil her for birthdays, Mother's Day, and especially at Christmas. I wanted to make up for all those years she'd gone without in the orphanage and foster home and raising children on her own.

One less pleasant issue had arisen shortly after my move to Virginia. I developed some recurrent sinus issues. When a doctor examined me, he brought up my broken nose. This was the first time I'd ever been told my nose had been broken. I instantly realized it must have happened the night Uncle Norman tried to murder me. Thankfully, the healed break wasn't noticeable, but it undoubtedly had contributed to my sinus problems.

I was still sharing my testimony whenever opportunity arose of how God had spared me from being murdered as a child, transformed my life when I came to Christ, and healed me from the negative effects of being sexually abused. More often than not, this was one-on-one. Sadly, many of those I shared with had their own story of childhood sexual abuse, sometimes telling it openly for the first time to me. I would tell them how God had given me a whole new life and could do the same for them. We usually ended our conversation with a prayer.

As I heard these stories from fellow victims, their abusers were almost always someone they trusted like their own father, a relative, dentist, scout leader, or priest. For the first time in my life, I felt compelled to tell the authorities what Uncle Norman had really done the night he tried to murder me and during years of prior sexual abuse. If I could have him imprisoned, it would at least ensure he could never harm another child.

Unsure of what to do, I decided to see a female Christian counselor. I hadn't been to one since my single visit to Ms. Samson twelve years earlier. Unlike that experience, I found myself eager to pour out my story to Ms. Lourdes. She asked to pray with me before we started, which I gladly welcomed.

After I told her my story, she suggested I keep a journal and prayed with me again before I left. From then on, I did begin keeping a journal, pouring out my memories and pain and thoughts and prayers to God. When I eventually began writing this book, I found my journal invaluable for chronicling accurately the details and emotions of those years.

Despite the good session, I found myself breaking into frenzied sobs as I drove home. I began to pray. "Dear heavenly Father, I thought I was healed from my painful childhood. I have a wonderful life now. I'm so grateful for your mercy towards me and for helping me forgive Uncle Norman. But I still want him imprisoned. It's the only way to ensure he won't hurt another child. He's like an albatross around my neck, and it seems I'll never be free of him. Please show me what to do!"

As I prayed, I realized that just because I'd forgiven Uncle Norman, that didn't prevent me from going to the police now. Calling Chrissy, I told her my plan.

"I want to try to put Uncle Norman in prison. If I can press charges against him for the sexual abuse and murder attempts, will you testify about what he did to you?"

"Absolutely," Chrissy responded.

When I told Wally and Mom about my plan, they were in complete agreement. I'd already decided not to tell my father since it had proved impossible to discuss Uncle Norman with him. I then called Uncle Ron to ask for Uncle Norman's most recent phone number.

"He's a severe alcoholic now," Uncle Ron informed me. "He's living with a friend in Arkansas, but I can give you his number."

I jotted down the number without saying why I wanted it. Later that evening, my father called.

"What's new?" he asked.

Had Uncle Ron told him I was asking for Uncle Norman's phone number? Was that why he'd called? I didn't want to tell him my plans, but now felt I had no choice. "I went to see a counselor about what Uncle Norman did to me. I'm going to see if I can press charges."

As always, my father's immediate response was in defense of his brother. "Sometimes it's better to let sleeping dogs lie. After all, Norman's sixty-two years old now and suffers with emphysema."

This wasn't what I wanted to hear. I eventually realized that my father responded to emotional pain the only way he knew how and exactly as I'd done for years—by burying it deep inside.

Jesus Christ had set me free, but my father remained trapped in the pain of his own neglected and abusive childhood. As Mom had done, I needed to see his faults with compassion.

But that didn't mean I would let my father change my course of action. I had now come up with my strategy. I would call Uncle Norman and get him to confess while I recorded our conversation. I could then use the recording as evidence to press charges.

CHAPTER TWENTY-EIGHT

This is a Recording

I know that I shall be justified.

—Job 13:18(b)

The following week my hands trembled as I attached the recording device to the telephone. It had been ten years since I'd called to tell Uncle Norman I forgave him. My heart beat rapidly as I dialed his number. The phone rang multiple times before a male finally answered.

"May I speak to Norman?" I asked.

"This is Norman," the voice responded.

"Well, this is your niece Mary."

"Oh, hi! My brother Ron told me you called him for my phone number. How are you doing?"

"I'm doing okay," I answered, surprised at my own calm demeanor.

"I heard you got married." My uncle sounded as though he was settling in for a normal conversation, but I wasn't interested in small talk.

"I have a lot of unanswered questions about what you did to me that I need to resolve. Have you ever told anyone what you did?"

"I told God."

"You told God? Well, God already knew because he saw everything," I retorted. "Are you sorry for what you did?"

"Of course! Of course!" His response sounded insincere, almost sarcastic.

"If you're sorry, why didn't you call me to apologize?" I demanded.

"I didn't know how to contact you."

What a lie! You could have gotten my phone number as easily as I got yours.

"Do you know why you tried to kill me?"

"I was on codeine."

What a lame excuse. I need to get a detailed confession.

"You know it was extremely traumatic for me to be sexually abused by you, forced to drink rat poison, smothered with a pillow, almost strangled to death, and then beaten with a hatchet," I said, still in a calm and controlled voice. "What do you have to say about that?"

He was quiet a moment, then muttered sullenly, "You're throwing too many questions at me."

"You know I told my family what you did. I wanted everyone to know the truth. What you did to me and my sister was sick too. You need to get help. I hope you're not doing that anymore!"

"I'm an old man now and an alcoholic."

Oh brother!

"Do you think just because it's been twenty-four years since you tried to murder me it's been forgotten?" I demanded.

"What did you say? I can't hear you. I think there's something wrong with the phone."

The next thing I heard was the dial tone.

Ugh! I wasn't finished!

I called back several times but always got a busy signal. When I played the recording back, the tape was blank. I couldn't understand what went wrong. I'd practiced several times beforehand to make sure it worked properly. The situation seemed hopeless without that evidence. Tears streamed down my face as I wondered what to do next.

If I can't get him off the streets and put in prison, I wish he'd feel so guilty he would do what Judas did and hang himself.

I didn't like these negative feelings. Getting out my journal, I began chronicling as I always did what had happened and how I felt about it. As I wrote, I also cried out my pain to God.

"Dear heavenly Father, I know you wanted me to forgive Uncle Norman, and I did that years ago. He deserves to be tormented in hell for what he did. He's never faced any consequences on earth, and he should have served time in prison. He doesn't even sound like he's sorry, and I don't know if he's harming any other children. Please forgive me and help me not to feel this way."

The next day I wrote the district attorney's office in the jurisdiction where the assault had occurred, requesting copies of any documents related to the second-degree assault charge against my uncle. Two weeks later, they arrived.

The first document I read was the investigator's report dated February 14, 1967, the morning of the interview. It described my injuries and stated that Uncle Norman had admitted to a felony second-degree assault charge. Attached to the report was the false statement I'd given. It was strange to read what I'd said and see my signature at the bottom of the page. I remembered the fear I'd experienced when I was questioned.

Mom's statement was also attached. She stated her relationship to my uncle and that he'd lived with us for a year prior to that day.

The rest of the documents were transcripts from the preliminary hearings. The bulk of the language consisted of dialogue between the attorneys for each side with a few comments from the judge and my uncle. Reading those documents was cathartic. Once I finished, I decided to send a second letter to the district attorney's office and presiding judge. I couldn't type it fast enough.

> *Dear Justice Daniels and District Attorney Redmond. I have enclosed a copy of transcripts as they relate to a case tried in your court in 1967 that involved myself when I was twelve years old, including the statement given to the New York State Police on February 14, 1967. The reason I am writing you today is to give you a true and accurate statement of what*

happened on February 13, 1967, when I was sexually assaulted, poisoned, smothered, strangled, beaten with a hatchet, and held against my will by my uncle, Norman Robarde. At that time, my uncle coerced me into not telling what really happened. In fear he was going to kill me if I told, I withheld the truth from the police, my family, and the courts for years until I was no longer afraid. The following is an accurate statement to the best of my recollection.

The letter continued for five pages and described the gory details. I couldn't remember the exact locations where my uncle took me that night, but I provided as much information as I could about the long trip on the same road where he took me to the motel, the pull-off area, the gas station, and the fast-food drive-in. I mentioned some of the road signs I recalled seeing that night.

I also told them I believed my uncle had only received probation because the authorities didn't know what actually transpired. I now wanted to press charges against my uncle for the crimes he hadn't been charged with. Though I was unsure of what their response might be, I was relieved to finally tell the authorities the truth after twenty-four years.

The following week, I received a phone call from Chief Investigator Williams in the district attorney's office. He told me he'd worked as a state trooper in the area for over twenty-five years and had been working there at the time of the assault. He said he knew the investigator who had questioned me, now retired. Investigator Williams was very interested in helping me if the statute of limitations permitted and would speak to the district attorney about my case.

"When would you be able to meet with us?" he finished.

It just so happened that I had already scheduled a trip to visit my family for the following month. Investigator Williams and I set a day and time to meet at his office. I could hardly wait!

CHAPTER TWENTY-NINE

Back to Reality

A man's heart deviseth his way; but the Lord directeth
his steps.

—Proverbs 16:9

W hen it was time to meet with the investigator and district
attorney, my stomach was full of butterflies. When I first
walked in, I was greeted by Investigator Williams. Tall with a slim
build and outgoing demeanor, he immediately made me feel
comfortable.

"Like I mentioned, I've worked this area for over twenty-five
years and know it well," he told me. "Why don't you take a ride
with me, and we'll see if we can retrace your steps that night. I'm
certain I can find each of the locations your uncle took you to."

I was doubtful but willing to give it a try. We soon pulled into
a parking lot in front a long one-story building that appeared to be
separated into twelve units.

"These are government-assisted apartment rentals," Investigator Williams said. "But this building was previously the Evergreen Motel. Does it look familiar at all?"

While I couldn't remember the name of the motel, Evergreen sounded familiar. Getting out of the car, I studied the building carefully. Though the once well-kept motel looked neglected and seedy, the overall structure was as I remembered. I immediately knew I was in the right place. I could feel an evil presence that seemed to inhabit the grounds.

As my memory flashed back to that night, my gaze darted to the left where the main office was located, then to the last room on the right where I'd almost been murdered. I turned to Investigator Williams, who was standing beside me.

"Yes, this is it. This is where he tried to rape me. Where he made me drink the poisoned alcohol. Where he tried to smother me to death."

Looking at the former motel brought the immeasurable horrors of that night into stark reality. I remembered my conversation three years earlier with my former pastor's wife Roberta when she'd sensed the Holy Spirit telling her I needed to accept what had happened to me. I now faced the reality of what I'd endured in that room.

It wasn't a nightmare.

It wasn't my imagination.

It was real!

Once again, I was overwhelmed with gratitude that I'd survived. *Dear heavenly Father, thank you for your mercy in sparing my life here that night.*

Getting back into the car, we continued on down the same road, this time in search of the pull-off area. Investigator Williams slowed the car as we approached a small area at an intersection. "Is this it?"

"No, this definitely isn't it. The area was larger, and it wasn't at an intersection. I also remember it was surrounded by trees on three sides."

Investigator Williams started driving again. "There's another spot up ahead."

We hadn't driven far when I spotted an area to the right. "That's it!"

The investigator immediately slowed down and pulled over. My heart was pounding so hard I thought it would come out of my chest. As I got out of the car, anxiety overwhelmed me. How strange to stand on the same spot where I was almost murdered. Once again I felt an evil presence.

Investigator Williams had now climbed out as well. He didn't say a word as I looked around. The area hadn't changed a bit in all those years. It was still a two-lane road surrounded by trees and foliage. Tears filled my eyes.

"This is where I fought for my life when he strangled me and beat me with the hatchet."

I wondered as I gazed into the densely wooded area if Uncle Norman had planned to chop up my body and bury me in those woods. Had anyone ever found the hatchet with my blood and hair on it? Or was it even now still embedded under the dirt from years of rain and snow?

I truly believed now that I'd wrestled with the devil himself on that hideous night. Miraculously he'd lost the fight. I found myself pouring my heart out silently to God.

Dear heavenly Father, thank you for your mercy in sparing my life that night. Thank you for your mercy towards my precious Mom and the rest of my family in sparing them such a horrible tragedy that would have affected them the rest of their lives. Thank you just doesn't seem adequate, but thank you, thank you, thank you!

I suddenly found Inspector Williams at my side. With concern in his voice, he asked. "Are you okay?"

I managed a smile. "I'm fine. I just can't believe I'm here after all these years."

We continued our journey, searching for the gas station where my uncle had taken me to clean up. A few minutes later, Investigator Williams pulled in front of a small convenience store. "I'm pretty sure this was the gas station."

"But there aren't any gas pumps," I pointed out.

"There used to be years ago."

Climbing out of the car, I looked around. "I distinctly remember my uncle brought me into a restroom on the far right side of the gas station."

Investigator Williams followed me as I walked around to the right side of the building. There I saw two door frames side by side but no doorknobs nor any sign above either door frame that might have read Ladies. As we got closer, I realized that the door frames had been sealed with painted sheets of plywood.

I searched for any indication there'd been a sign over either door frame that had been removed. Then I saw it. Barely visible beneath a coat of white paint was a single word above the door frame on the right—Ladies.

"This is definitely it," I said, my heart pounding again as I recalled the reflection of my bloody face in the mirror. "This was where he made me wash the blood off my face and hands."

Getting back in the car, we continued in search of the fast-food drive-in. We soon pulled into an empty parking lot with a boarded-up building. The telephone booth was still where I remembered it.

"Yes, this is where he bought me the food I threw out the car window. The phone booth there is where he made the calls to Mom and the police."

I looked over at Investigator Williams. "Thank you for taking the time to locate the sites for me. It's amazing you worked here years ago and knew how to find them. I never even thought to look for them. Even if I did, I wouldn't have been able to locate them myself."

Now that we'd confirmed each of the four locations, I was confident this would help my case. Returning to the office, Investigator Williams and I met with District Attorney Donald Redmond. I reiterated my story to both of them. Investigator Williams informed me that if I'd waited one more year, the file of my case might not have been there since they were destroyed after twenty-five years.

"Did you find the Polaroid photograph the investigator took of me?" I asked.

Investigator Williams shook his head. "It wasn't in the file."

"Are you sure? I specifically remember the investigator took my picture with a Polaroid camera."

"I'm sorry, but there was no photograph."

Disappointment set in. Was it possible the film just hadn't developed properly for some reason? After all, I'd never actually seen the developed print. In any case, maybe it was better if I didn't see my battered image from that night, or it might have haunted me even more than my memories had already.

I looked over at the district attorney. "Is there anything I can do to press charges against my uncle for the actual crimes he committed against me? Crimes I was threatened to tell no one about?"

The district attorney explained that because my uncle had been charged with second-degree assault, he could not be charged with any other crime related to the events of that day due to the laws pertaining to double jeopardy. In addition, the statute of limitations had run out on those crimes.

"But I was only a child, and I was forced to lie," I protested. "There must be something I can do!"

The district attorney apologized for the situation I was in but reiterated there was nothing I could do.

"What about the sexual abuse that went on for years? Can I at least press charges for those crimes?" I asked, trying to remain calm.

The district attorney explained that the statute of limitations had run out on those crimes long ago. I choked back tears as the bad news sunk in. It didn't seem fair. At thirty-six years old, I'd finally had the courage to come forward, but it was too late.

Investigator Williams apologized again that nothing could be done.

"I understand," I said. "I appreciate all you did for me."

I shook their hands and thanked them for their time, then headed back to Chrissy's with mixed emotions. On the one hand, I actually felt better after revisiting each of the sites. I felt God had wanted me to retrace my steps and had brought me to those places when he knew I could handle it. To me, it was no coincidence Investigator Williams had worked as a state trooper in the area during that time period. Nor was it a coincidence but part of God's healing process that he'd been able to locate each of the sites.

On the other hand, I was deeply disappointed I couldn't press charges. Arriving back at Chrissy's house, I told her and Mom what happened, then called Wally.

"I wonder why the district attorney and investigator agreed to meet with me," I questioned aloud. "They knew I couldn't press charges for attempted murder because of double jeopardy, and they knew the statute of limitations expired. They could have easily informed me of that on the phone."

Wally didn't have any answers to that either. I could only trust that God had prompted them to meet with me in person so that Investigator Williams could in turn guide me to the scenes of the crime.

The following week after returning to our home in northern Virginia, I was flipping through TV channels when I came across a program featuring staff from a local craft store who were making jewelry. In mere seconds, I knew I wanted to make jewelry. I signed up for classes, began making beaded jewelry, and was soon selling my wares at work, local craft shows, and in gift shops. I came to realize the healing I'd received from revisiting the scenes of the crime had released a creativity I never knew was in me.

But as the years continued to pass, I still couldn't accept the fact that I was unable to press further charges against Uncle Norman or make sure no other child would ever be harmed by him. I needed a new plan.

CHAPTER THIRTY

Wrestling with God

And we know that all things work together for good to
them that love God.

—Romans 8:28(a)

I contacted a friend in New York, who in turn referred me to a
good lawyer. Calling the law office, I scheduled a phone
consultation. In advance, I sent copies of the transcripts from my
1967 case and the five-page letter I'd sent to the district attorney.
When the time came for our scheduled consultation, I called with
confidence that the lawyer would be able to help me. Instead, he
reiterated what I'd heard from the district attorney.

"I'm sorry to tell you, but the statute of limitations has run out
on any charges of sexual abuse or any other charges for that
matter. Nor will you be able to press charges for the murder
attempts due to double jeopardy. There's nothing you can do."

The lawyer sounded genuinely sympathetic. I called Wally to
break the news. "I can't believe that the laws won't allow me to do

anything. This is absolutely ridiculous! How is a survivor ever supposed to press charges if the window of opportunity is so narrow that by the time they are finally emotionally able to come forward it's too late to do anything?"

Though deeply disappointed, I still felt the need to do something. Writing a letter to the chief of police in the county where my uncle lived, I related what Uncle Norman had done to me and Chrissy. I suggested they keep an eye on him to make sure he wasn't around other children. I then mailed the letter and left the outcome in God's hands, praying that Uncle Norman would never harm another child.

About this same time, God began impressing on my heart that I needed to pray for Uncle Norman to come to Christ so that he too could find forgiveness from God. But I couldn't bring myself to pray for my uncle. In truth, I didn't think he deserved God's mercy.

What I didn't realize was that my inability to pray for Uncle Norman was the final link in the chain that kept me in bondage to him. From the Bible, I'd learned that God was so merciful he didn't want anyone to go to hell. He would forgive anyone who was truly sorry for what they'd done and asked for God's forgiveness. They would then be free from the punishment of hell and ultimately go to heaven. I loved telling others about the forgiveness God offers and the personal relationship they can have with Jesus Christ. I wanted everyone to know this was available to them.

That is, everyone except Uncle Norman. If I prayed for Uncle Norman and he did become truly repentant, this meant his slate would be wiped clean in God's eyes. It was hard for me to accept he could escape punishment in the afterlife in addition to the punishment he escaped here on earth.

God continued to impress upon me I was to pray for my uncle, but I ignored the promptings. Instead, I argued with God. "Lord, wasn't it enough I dealt with him here on earth? Do I have to see him in heaven too?"

A Bible character I could especially relate to was Joseph, whose story is told in the book of Genesis. Joseph was just seventeen when his brothers plotted to kill him. One brother managed to talk the others into selling Joseph instead into slavery. Joseph eventually became head slave in charge of his master's house, then was falsely accused of rape by his master's wife and sent to prison.

During Joseph's imprisonment, God gave him the ability to interpret dreams, first for other prisoners, then for the Pharaoh, Egypt's ruler, giving warning of an upcoming famine and a plan to save Egypt from starvation. Pharaoh was so impressed he elevated Joseph to second-in-command after Pharaoh himself.

A few years later when the famine began, Joseph's brothers went to Egypt to buy wheat. They didn't recognize Joseph, whom they'd sold into slavery twenty-two years earlier, but Joseph recognized them. When he revealed his true identity, they were terrified he would take revenge. But Joseph responded:

> Now therefore be not grieved, nor angry with
> yourselves, that ye sold me hither; for God did send me
> before you . . . to preserve you a posterity in the earth,
> and to save your lives by a great deliverance.
> (Genesis 45:5-7)

The brothers intended evil toward Joseph, but God used what they'd done to save the Israelites as well as Egypt and other nations so they wouldn't perish when famine hit the land. As I read this story again and again, I began wondering if God could also bring good out of the evil of my own traumatic childhood.

"Dear heavenly Father," I prayed. "I ask that you bring good out of the evil that happened to me just as you did in Joseph's life. I don't know what good could possibly come out of it, but all things are possible with you. Just show me what it is you want me to do."

Could God be calling me to try to change New York law on the statute of limitations regarding sexual abuse crimes against children? Many states have no such statute of limitations, but in New York State, there was an unreasonably small window of time for victims to press charges. And since most victims of childhood sexual abuse are unable to talk about their experiences well into adulthood, if ever, by the time they are emotionally able to press charges against their abusers, the legal timeline prohibits them from doing so.

If I could help change the law, that would definitely be something good to help other victims. Contacting my former boss Patrick, who had become a close, lifelong friend, I explained, "I want to change the New York State statute of limitations on sexual abuse crimes against children. Could you set up a website for me to find other childhood sexual abuse victims interested in changing the law?"

Patrick agreed to help. During my lunch break and in the evenings, I made phone calls, did research, and wrote letters. I contacted others I knew were victims and asked them to send me their stories. The task felt monumental, and my efforts proved fruitless. I realized I didn't have the manpower or time to dedicate to such a venture while working a full-time job. A year after starting my campaign, I abandoned the project.

Sometime earlier, a friend had recommended several Christian books on emotional healing from childhood abuse, including *The Bondage Breaker* by Dr. Neil T. Anderson, *Freeing Your Mind From Memories That Bind* by Fred and Florence Littauer, and *A Door of Hope* by Jan Frank. Frustrated with my inability to have my uncle imprisoned or change the statute of limitations, I began reading these books. Some of them were testimonies from other women abused as children who had found healing. Others discussed how to find freedom from bondage to one's negative past.

The books provided me with new insights. I learned that victims of child sexual abuse can have various negative emotions including anger, shame, low self-esteem, loneliness, worthlessness, despair, hopelessness, bitterness, depression, and anxiety. They often feel ugly and dirty or like damaged goods. They also exhibit behaviors such as rage, substance abuse, eating disorders, promiscuity, prostitution, poor relationship choices, perfectionism, controlling behavior, and other dysfunctional conduct.

I recognized my former self in many of these negative emotions and actions. I could now understand why I'd felt as I did for many years and why I'd behaved as I did in my early twenties. As I read and re-read these books, I came to peace with the reality that I couldn't have Uncle Norman imprisoned or change the statute of limitations. Once I accepted those facts, I was finally able to put my past behind me.

But I still couldn't bring myself to pray for Uncle Norman.

CHAPTER THIRTY-ONE

Family Matters

The effectual fervent prayer of a righteous man availeth much.

—James 5:16

I continued to pray for Wally and do all I could to be a Christian example to him. I was also still making and selling my jewelry as a hobby. Then four years after we married, Wally's sister Susie was diagnosed with an aggressive form of cancer. That same year Wally's father was diagnosed with congestive heart failure.

Sometime later, Wally and I were staying in New York City for a few nights as we customarily did on our way home from visiting my family. We loved to attend the musical theater, dine at great restaurants, and visit with friends. When we got back to our hotel room, I tuned in to *The 700 Club*. With the recent illnesses of his father and sister, death and eternity were at the forefront of Wally's thoughts, and after the program we began discussing them. That night Wally prayed to accept Christ as his Savior. When we returned home, he began attending church with me and was eventually baptized.

Three months later, Susie called to inform us their father had passed away at home in his sleep. The soonest I could book a flight to Los Angeles was two days later. Susie, who was still battling cancer, would make the funeral arrangements and take care of things until we arrived.

We had a layover in Pittsburgh, but when we arrived, we discovered that our next flight had been delayed due to a cracked windshield in the plane's cockpit. We waited for hours before the airline finally made an announcement.

"For passengers booked on Flight 1321 to Los Angeles, the flight has been cancelled. Flight 466 is taking passengers on a first-come, first-serve basis, leaving out of Gate 3A in forty-five minutes."

Before the announcement was finished, a stampede had broken out.

"I'll stay with the bags," Wally shouted. "Go!"

By the time I reached Gate 3A, at least twenty people were in line ahead of me. When Wally arrived with our bags, I waved him to join me.

"We need to say a quick prayer." Leaning in close to Wally, I prayed in a low voice, "Dear heavenly Father, please make a way for us to get on this flight."

As the line crept closer to the ticket counter, I heard the airline representative tell a woman in front of us that the flight was full.

Finally it was our turn. Handing over our tickets, I asked, "Is this flight fully booked?"

"Yes." The ticket agent had his head down as he typed away into the computer. I assumed he was looking up available flights.

"When is the next flight to L.A.?"

"At 5:00 p.m., but that's full also. The next available flight is tomorrow." The agent's head was still down as he worked busily behind the counter. It looked as though he was printing out a set of tickets.

"But we can't stay overnight in Pittsburgh," I protested, deeply discouraged. "My father-in-law just died. We have to get to L.A. for the funeral. Could you see if there might be two people willing to give up their seats for us?"

The agent finally looked up at me. "Oh, you're already booked on this flight."

I was stunned. "Really? Who booked our seats?"

"I don't know, but you're all set." With a smile, the agent handed me the tickets he'd been printing out. Goosebumps rose on my arms as I saw my name and Wally's on them.

I looked over at Wally, tears flooding my eyes. "Now that was an amazing answer to prayer!"

We stayed in L.A. until the funeral, then flew back home. Just six months later, Susie's battle with cancer deteriorated. Since she had no remaining family close by, Wally and I took leaves of absence from our jobs and flew to California to care for her. Like Wally, Susie had left her Catholic upbringing long ago and for years had attended a New Age church. While we were there, I was able to share my faith with her. Six weeks after we arrived, Susie accepted Christ as her Savior.

Susie's health worsened rapidly over the next few weeks. Late one night, I was lying on the bed beside Susie, reading scriptures to her about heaven. Minutes later, she stepped into God's presence. After a memorial service, Wally and I again headed back home.

The following year, I was on the internet browsing through *The 700 Club* website when I noticed a little comment box that said, "Tell us your story." The moment I saw it, I remembered that evening twelve years earlier when I'd been watching the show and sensed God telling me that one day I would share my own story on their show.

Without hesitation, I typed a couple brief paragraphs, telling how God had spared me from being murdered, healed me from childhood sexual abuse, answered my prayers for a husband, and transformed my life. Then I grabbed the mouse and clicked the SEND button.

CHAPTER THIRTY-TWO

The Long Search

The things which are impossible with men are possible with God.

—Luke 18:27

N ow seventy-one, Mom was down from New York on one of her semi-annual visits when she brought up the mother she'd never known.

"I would love to have a picture of my mother," she said wistfully. "The only one I owned was ruined while I was still at St. Cecilia's. I always kept it in the pocket of my uniform and put it in the wash one day by mistake. I've wanted a new one ever since."

It wasn't unusual for Mom to mention her mother, especially on Mother's Day. But she'd been doing so more often. Some years earlier, she'd learned from a distant cousin that her mother had passed away during my own childhood. Over the years, she'd occasionally mentioned her siblings, especially those who had been in the foster home with her. She'd told us stories about her childhood. But in all that she'd never said a negative word about her mother, who'd visited her only once.

I don't know why I never pressed Mom further about her family. Nor why I never attempted to locate them, especially since it had bothered me for years how Mom ended up in an orphanage and her family was separated. In truth, I hadn't thought about it since I became a Christian.

But I would do anything for Mom and was determined to make up for the hardship of her earlier years. Her longing for a picture of her own mother impelled me to find one. I decided to look for Mom's family and find out how she'd ended up in St. Cecilia's. Finding a fresh notebook and pen, I sat down with her.

"Mom, I'm going to help you find a photo of your mother and your family too. But I need as much information as you can give me. Do you know when and where your mother was born? Her maiden name? Your siblings' names? When they were born? The names of any aunts and uncles?"

By the time I finished hammering Mom with questions, she was exhausted, but I had enough data to start. Over the next few months, I searched the internet for anyone with my maternal grandmother's maiden name and my maternal grandfather's last name. I found some relatives in Upstate New York where my mother's family had been living before they were separated. I made numerous phone calls to distant relatives and in-laws of relatives. This produced some information, but no photographs.

Sadly, I discovered over time that three of Mom's five siblings were deceased, leaving only her older sister Agnes and her younger brother Frank. Locating an address for Agnes, I wrote her several letters explaining that I was working on my genealogy and wanted to meet her. I also made clear that my family was doing well financially and that we weren't looking for anything except to meet her and copy any photographs she might have of her mother.

Agnes didn't respond to my letters, which didn't surprise Mom. The last time Mom had spoken to her older sister was when she'd called to let Agnes know she'd just given birth to Chrissy and me. Agnes had told Mom never to call her again since she'd told her boss and co-workers she didn't have any family.

Mom hadn't seen her brother Frank since he'd showed up at her home intoxicated when I was a child. Several distant relatives told me they'd heard he passed away. I couldn't locate a death certificate, so I began searching the internet for nursing homes in the area where they grew up.

Calling the first nursing home on my list, I told the receptionist, "I'm trying to locate my uncle, Frank Bouchand. Would anyone by that name be living there?"

"One moment, I'll check." There was a pause. Then the receptionist came back on the line. "Yes, we have a Frank Bouchand."

"You do?" That I'd located my uncle on the very first call was truly amazing. It could only be another answer to prayer. "Could you connect me to his room?"

The receptionist transferred me to a nurse who explained that Uncle Frank had been living there since a stroke a few years earlier. She connected me to his room.

"Uncle Frank, this is your sister Marie's daughter," I introduced myself. "I'm Mary, one of the twins. We've been looking for you."

His garbled speech was difficult to understand, but I was able to catch the gist of it. We both cried during our conversation. I told him Mom wanted to see him. When I called Mom to tell her the news, she was ecstatic.

Shortly thereafter, Wally and I traveled to Upstate New York to meet my uncle. Mom joined us, and we drove together over to the nursing home. There wasn't a dry eye as we crowded into Uncle Frank's room that day. Mom reminisced about how, when she was five, she'd pushed Frank in his carriage and how she'd sat with him under the apple tree when they were at the foster home.

We also explained to Uncle Frank about my search for a photo of their mother. But he didn't have one either. Mom and I both promised to keep in touch and visit him.

It was while Mom and I were working on our genealogy that Mom began opening up about the horrible things she'd suffered during her nine years with the Blackburns. Like soaking Mom's fingers in kerosene and forcing her to suck on them if she wet the bed. Or being made to kneel for hours on raw beans with her arms raised to the sides as a punishment. The foster children were often fed just bread and butter while the Blackburns ate normal meals.

Other stories of abuse were very difficult for me to hear. Mom was raped twice while at the Blackburns, once by a neighborhood boy and once by the boyfriend of the Blackburns' biological daughter. By age fourteen, Mom could no longer take the abuse. She and Agnes walked to a neighbor's house to call social services. Within a short time, they'd been placed back at the Catholic orphanage.

"I'm so sorry you went through all that," I told Mom. My heart ached for her, but it seemed therapeutic for her to finally open up about her own traumatic childhood. I could now see that she'd walked her own journey from trauma and pain and grief to redemption in Christ, just as I had.

Meanwhile, I had continued my search for a photo of my maternal grandmother. I finally found her only living sibling, Fay. The youngest of her family, Fay was now eighty-two years old. Even she didn't have a photo of her older sister.

By now I'd learned that my maternal grandmother's parents were first generation Italian immigrants while my maternal grandfather's family had immigrated from France to Canada, then to the United States. My grandmother had given birth to six children in six years, all by the age of twenty-four. After my maternal grandfather abandoned my grandmother and their six children during the Depression, she had no means to support them so was forced to place them in foster homes and orphanages.

I never discovered why Mom's parents didn't keep in touch with their children. But Mom did find out that her mother had showed up at St. Cecilia's one day with the intention of taking

Mom home with her. The nun in charge had insisted Mom was better off at the orphanage and talked my grandmother into leaving her there.

I was able to locate all but one of my first cousins. None of them had met any of their parent's siblings, and their parents rarely spoke of their sad childhoods. Some of them had heard about my mom as the aunt who became a nun. Over the next eighteen months, I located some second cousins who shared stories and photographs, but still no picture of my grandmother.

"Dear Lord, please help me," I prayed. "You know about Mom's sad and lonely childhood. She's endured so much. She wants a photograph of her mother so badly. If there is one out there, you know where it is, so please make it known to me."

Not long after, I received a phone call from a distant cousin who had heard I was working on my genealogy. She'd been tracing our family history for years and had interesting stories to share. She promised to mail me a CD (compact disc) containing family photographs and documentation back to the eighteen hundreds.

She also faxed me one of the photographs. I immediately called Mom. "I'm looking at a beautiful photograph of your mother!"

"You are?" Mom could not contain her excitement. "What is it like? Oh, I wish I could see it!"

"I'll send you a copy right away. It's a professional studio photograph taken at a wedding when your mother was sixteen. One of her older sisters is the bride and your mother is the maid of honor. She's wearing a beautiful lacy dress. She actually looks a lot like me."

It was an amazing thing to be finally looking at the woman who had given birth to Mom over seventy years before. The very next day, I printed a copy and mailed it to Mom. As soon as I could, I had a more professional print made and framed for her. Mom carried that picture everywhere, showing it to her friends.

By the end of my search, I had an entire album of family photographs, including my great-grandparents, grandparents, aunts, uncles, and cousins. I eventually found at least one photo of each of Mom's siblings. The one photograph I located of my maternal grandfather was of his First Communion. The album also included birth and death certificates, ship logs, orphanage records, school records, baptismal records, stories about family members, and other miscellaneous records from the eighteen hundreds right up to the present.

I eventually organized a reunion for all the family members I'd located. At the reunion I gave each of my first cousins framed photos of the grandparents we'd never known. That Christmas, I presented Mom and Chrissy with copies of the entire album.

"How do you feel now?" I asked my mom.

"I feel free!" she responded. This entire search had been an incredible healing experience for Mom, especially finding the photos of her mother and other family members. God was restoring Mom from her painful past just as he had restored me.

For me too, it had been a blessing to learn how Mom had ended up in the orphanage and the whereabouts of her family. I'd started out asking God for a photo of my grandmother. But he gave me so much more. From not knowing where Mom came from, I now knew my own lineage back to the eighteen hundreds.

On my next trip to New York, I traveled up to visit Uncle Frank. Mom continued sending him cards and visiting him. He passed away just a year later, and I was so thankful Mom had been able to restore a relationship with her brother before it was too late.

CHAPTER THIRTY-THREE

All Over the World

Whatsoever ye have spoken in darkness shall be heard in the light.

—Luke 12:3(a)

A few weeks later after dinner, I went upstairs to our office to check my personal email. Moments later, I ran excitedly downstairs to tell Wally the news. "Remember when I told you I submitted my testimony to *The 700 Club* four years ago? They just replied and want to air my story!"

It had been sixteen years since I sensed God tell me I would one day share my testimony on their show. Petrified of public speaking, I asked God to help me overcome my shyness so that I could give hope to others.

The 700 Club sent a news team to our home to interview me. When the camera began rolling in our living room, I felt a supernatural peace fall over me. Before I knew it, the interview was over. After my story aired, I received many phone calls and emails with positive feedback from family members and friends.

A few days later, I received an email from the producer, letting me know that thousands of people had called the show for prayer after my segment aired. Many had shared about their own dark secrets, and almost two hundred had prayed to receive Jesus Christ. It was such a huge response that my interview had been chosen to be dubbed in Spanish for the Spanish-language version of their show.

The positive responses were an answer to my many years of praying when I had asked God to bring good out of what the devil meant for evil.

The following year, I was listening to one of my favorite Christian radio programs on my way to work. The program's host, Dr. James Dobson, a minister and psychologist, was interviewing a man who had sexually abused several underage boys years before. He was imprisoned for his crimes and became a Christian while incarcerated. After his release, he started a ministry to help other men break free from those abnormal compulsions.

Dr. Dobson mentioned that child abuse victims long to have their abusers apologize to them. Unfortunately, many never get to hear those words. He asked his guest if he would become a surrogate abuser for a few minutes and apologize to any listeners who were sexual abuse victims and never received an apology.

The guest speaker agreed and began to speak. "I know I have caused you a lot of pain, and I caused you to fear."

His apology was brief but powerful. It is almost impossible to put into words how I felt as he spoke. It was as if I was truly hearing an apology from my uncle. I wiped tears from my face as I listened to the rest of the interview.

"Dear heavenly Father, thank you for giving me the apology I longed to receive."

On my lunch break, I called the Christian radio program and the surrogate abuser's ministry and left messages to tell them how God had used that interview to minister to me. After that experience, I no longer needed an apology from my uncle.

As hard as it was for me to accept, the interview also taught me that God extends his forgiveness to everyone, even those who commit crimes against children, if they are truly repentant. The interview was a demonstration of 2 Peter 3:9:

> The Lord is not slack concerning his promise, as some men count slackness; but is longsuffering to us-ward, not willing that any should perish, but that all should come to repentance.

I journaled about the interview and told Wally, Mom, and Chrissy about it. Chrissy listened to the interview for herself and got the idea to write Uncle Norman a letter as she wanted Uncle Norman to apologize to me directly. But she didn't carry through with her idea at this time and soon forgot about it.

After that radio interview, I wondered about the young man who had sexually assaulted me thirty years earlier before my graduation from Katharine Gibbs. I wanted to tell him I forgave him. Dredging up his name from my memory, I searched for him online. It wasn't long before I found an obituary indicating he'd passed away two years earlier. I was somewhat disappointed but also relieved I didn't have to speak to him.

The following year we went back to France on vacation. Since Wally's sister lived there, we tried to visit every year or so and enjoyed exploring different regions. One year we'd even participated in a mission trip to northern France, where Wally and I helped restore a sixteenth century chateau that was being used as an international prayer center, stripping wallpaper, painting, landscaping, and other tasks.

As soon as we arrived home from our flight back to the United States, I checked my email and discovered one from the producer of *The 700 Club*. They wanted to re-tape part of my interview, make it more of a Christmas story, and re-air the second version. A short time later, their news team returned to our home, which was decorated for Christmas, and re-taped part of the segment.

After the second version aired, the producer emailed to let me know there'd been such a huge response they'd decided to air my story internationally. I was overwhelmed and amazed to see the very secret I'd been forced to keep all those years now being broadcast all over the world to touch and change lives. God was using my redemption journey to do more than I could ever have dreamed, and I had full faith and confidence that lives would be transformed and hurting hearts receive hope in every time zone and people group across the planet where my story was televised.

The good that came from *The 700 Club* broadcasts and the surrogate abuser's interview enabled me for the first time to pray for Uncle Norman's salvation. In the ten years I'd resisted God's promptings to pray for my uncle, I'd thought he was the only one who would benefit from those prayers. But once I finally prayed for Uncle Norman, I felt the chains that bound me to him were broken at last.

A few years later, a scripture passage spoke to me as I read how Judas had made his choice to betray Jesus:

> Now the Feast of Unleavened Bread drew nigh, which is called the Passover. And the chief priests and scribes sought how they might kill him; for they feared the people. Then entered Satan into Judas surnamed Iscariot, being of the number of the twelve. And he went his way, and communed with the chief priests and captains, how he might betray him unto them. And they were glad, and covenanted to give him money. And he promised, and sought opportunity to betray him unto them in the absence of the multitude. (Luke 22:1-6)

After I read that story, I realized that the scripture said Satan literally entered Judas. I realized my real enemy was not Uncle Norman. My real enemy was Satan. Uncle Norman was simply the instrument Satan had used to try to destroy me. That didn't exonerate Uncle Norman's criminal behavior. His bad choices allowed him to be used that way, just as Judas allowed Satan to use him. But it did help me understand things on a more spiritual level.

As I thought about the possibility of Uncle Norman becoming a Christian, I envisioned myself grabbing my uncle by his ankles as the devil tried to pull him through the gates of hell and yanking him out of Satan's clutches.

CHAPTER THIRTY-FOUR

The Unexpected

Blessed are they that mourn for they shall be comforted.
—Matthew 5:4

M y father was in his early eighties when he was diagnosed with congestive heart failure and other health issues. Chrissy helped take care of him when Sylvia wasn't there, and I called weekly to check on him. One day when I called Mom to update her on my father's health, she told me she'd just come back from the emergency room.

"What happened?" I asked with immediate concern.

"Well, I've been feeling weak and nauseous. They said I have a urinary tract infection."

The next day, I called to check on her.

"I still feel sick," she said. "I can't eat a thing."

"Do you want me to come up there?" I asked. "I know Chrissy is out of town."

"No, I'll be okay."

The next day I received a frantic call from Chrissy. "Mom's having a heart attack. I just got back in town, and I knew something was wrong as soon as I saw her. We're in the emergency room now."

The ER staff confirmed that Mom was in the middle of a heart attack. Traveling up to New York, I camped out in Mom's hospital room for the duration of her stay. Chrissy came every day. Once she was back home, I began looking for someone to help care for Mom since Chrissy and I both had to return to our jobs. I found a nice young woman to cook, clean, and do errands as needed, which permitted Mom to return to her own home and life.

That summer Chrissy completed her doctoral studies, and received her PhD in Health Education. We were all so proud of her. I returned to New York several months later for Mom's eightieth birthday. She seemed back to her former self. My father was in the hospital at the time, and Mom expressed a desire to visit him. Much to our amazement, he agreed. Chrissy and I were both present. It was wonderful to see them together after so many years. My father even allowed Chrissy and me to take a few photos of them together.

A few weeks before Christmas, I called Mom one Saturday afternoon. She was decorating a Christmas tree and sounded her usual cheerful self. I called her again the next day, but she didn't pick up. I left several messages, then called again early Monday morning before work. When she still didn't answer, I sensed something was wrong.

Since Mom hadn't given anyone an extra key to her apartment, I called the office manager of her building to do a welfare check. The manager called back a few minutes later to tell me that Mom had passed away peacefully while sitting in her rocking chair. It was later determined she'd died from cardiac arrest.

Distraught, I could hardly hold myself together to listen to the manager's words. I immediately traveled to New York to begin planning Mom's funeral arrangements and obituary with Chrissy. This included a beautiful biography of her life that we wrote up and was published in the local newspaper. Her funeral was held at St. Mark's the day after the most severe ice storm to hit Upstate New York in two decades. Despite the bad weather, a large number whose lives she'd touched in the community were in attendance.

While I knew Mom was in heaven and I would see her again someday, her loss devastated me. She was both mother and father all those years my father wasn't around, best friend, prayer partner, and encourager. Wally couldn't comfort me, and neither could anyone else.

I eventually went to a healing service. As my brothers and sisters in Christ prayed over me, God instantly relieved me from my intense emotional pain. But I still missed our wonderful times together and especially the love she had for me.

A month after our mother's funeral, Chrissy called to tell me our father was back in the hospital. "The doctor says he has only a couple more days."

I wasn't surprised our eighty-four-year-old father's health had been deteriorating over the past year. In truth, I was surprised he'd lived as long as he did. But I'd been hoping not to receive this call so soon after Mom's death.

I arrived in New York the next evening. Sylvia and Chrissy were there. The next day a priest was called in, and we all prayed with my father. He passed away early the next morning. A few days later we had a small military service for him. Less than fifteen people were in attendance, more than I'd expected since my father had lived like a recluse most of his life.

Three weeks after my father's passing, Chrissy and I were emailing back and forth when she shared that the Holy Spirit had told her Uncle Norman didn't have long to live. This had given her a new urgency to see Uncle Norman apologize to me. She'd written a letter to Uncle Norman, asking him to call me and apologize, and had emailed the letter to Sylvia, asking her to make sure Uncle Norman received it.

I was surprised by Chrissy's actions, but didn't expect a response from Uncle Norman since he hadn't apologized when I'd called him years earlier. Since I'd already received the surrogate apology from that Christian radio interview, I really didn't feel I needed another one. I told Chrissy I was fine with whatever happened and promptly forgot about it.

CHAPTER THIRTY-FIVE

The Phone Call

For by grace are ye saved through faith.

—Ephesians 2:8(a)

I was backing into my driveway when my cell phone rang. It was Sylvia. She'd called several times since my father's passing for one thing or another, so I didn't think it unusual.

"Are you okay?" she asked. It seemed an odd question.

"I'm just getting home from work. Why?"

"Well, you're about to get a call. Your Uncle Norman just tried to call a couple of times, but didn't leave any messages."

"Uncle Norman?"

"Didn't your sister tell you?"

"Tell me what?"

"She felt your Uncle Norman didn't have much time left and wanted him to apologize to you before he passed away. A few days ago, she asked me to give him her letter."

"Yes, she told me that, but I didn't expect Uncle Norman to respond."

"Well, he wants to speak to you. Will you talk to him?"

"Of course."

"I'll call him back now," Sylvia said excitedly, "and let him know you're home before he changes his mind!"

My stomach turned queasy as I walked into the house. I hadn't spoken to my uncle since I'd called him eighteen years earlier, surreptitiously trying to record our conversation as evidence to imprison him.

"Dear heavenly Father," I prayed aloud, "when my Uncle Norman calls, please have the Holy Spirit take over our conversation."

Seconds later, the phone rang. It was Uncle Norman. He was sobbing. "M-a-a-a-r-y?"

"Yes?" Surprisingly, I was not emotional at all but felt complete peace.

"I'm so sorry!" His voice had a sincerity that was foreign to me.

"I know. It's okay. I forgive you."

"I've wanted to call you for years, but I was too scared. When I received your sister's letter, I asked God to give me the strength to call. I've been a nervous wreck all day trying to get up enough courage."

It had been forty-two years since Uncle Norman tried to murder me. He was unaware I no longer needed his apology. In fact, by this point his apology was more for him than for me, though he didn't realize that either.

"Well, I think you're very courageous," I consoled him. "Not too many people in your position would do this."

I went on to share how I'd lived a wild lifestyle for years in my twenties, how God had forgiven me for things I did and healed me emotionally. "I was very angry with you for many years, but I'm not anymore."

"You had every right to be angry," he responded sadly.

"I'm very happy now," I said. "I have a wonderful husband. We've been married for almost nineteen years. God has given me a life I never thought possible."

"I've asked God at least a thousand times to forgive me."

"You must believe in him then?" I asked.

"Of course!" my uncle said.

"And you know he's forgiven you?"

"I hope so."

"I know God will forgive you and give you peace just as he did for me. Have you ever committed your life to Jesus and received the forgiveness God offers when you accept what Christ did when he gave his life for you on the cross?"

"No," he said.

"Well, the gift of forgiveness Jesus offers is free to anyone who asks. We don't have to pay for it. It's nothing we can earn. It's all about believing and receiving what he has provided for us."

I went on to share the same gospel message Jean had shared with me almost thirty years earlier and I had shared with Wally and others over the years. "Would you like to pray with me now to receive Jesus Christ into your life as your Lord and Savior? I don't want you to feel pressured to do this. I only want you to do this if you really want to."

"I want to!" Uncle Norman sounded very sincere.

While we were speaking, I rummaged around for a Christian pamphlet someone had given me that I knew contained a simple example of praying to accept Christ as Savior. Finding it, I flipped to the right page.

"Uncle Norman, I have a prayer here I'm going to read. If you agree with the words, just repeat them after me until we finish the entire prayer. Does that sound okay?"

"Yes."

I read a portion of the prayer. Then he repeated it. Once again, I could hear the sincerity in his voice. We continued until we had both recited the entire prayer. Then I finished, "In Jesus's name, amen."

"In Jesus's name, amen," he repeated.

We chatted for a few more minutes as I tried to make sure he'd understood and meant what he'd prayed. He seemed very genuine and sure, so I went on to ask if he lived near a church. He explained that he was hooked up to a portable oxygen tank due to his emphysema and couldn't get around easily.

"What about a Bible?" I asked. "Do you have one?"

"I have an old one."

"Have you ever read it?"

"No. It's too difficult to understand."

"I can order you one that's easy to understand and in large print. I'll order it tomorrow."

"How much will it cost?"

"I can usually find them at a good price. In any case, this is my gift to you."

Uncle Norman didn't know that since I'd become a Christian, giving someone their first Bible was one of my favorite things to do. I usually ordered them in bulk or bought them at thrift stores. We argued amicably for several minutes as to who would pay for the Bible. I won.

Uncle Norman then asked if he could send me money every month to give to my church.

"No, no, no," I responded. I knew he had only a meager social security pension. "You need your money."

"I like to help the poor," he argued back.

"But you *are* the poor."

We both chuckled. I couldn't believe I'd actually laughed with the person who'd been my tormenter for so many years. It boggled my mind. At one point during our conversation, I actually called him Uncle Norman.

"I haven't heard anyone call me that in many years," he said emotionally. "It's nice to hear."

Uncle Norman had been estranged from most of his family except my father and Sylvia for many years. This included nieces or nephews who could refer to him as uncle. For me too, calling him Uncle Norman was healing because I'd avoided saying his name due to the painful memories.

As we wound up our phone call, Uncle Norman asked, "Can I call you again in a few months?"

"A few months? No, I'll call you next week."

Since he couldn't make it to church, I was his only source of spiritual guidance. I wanted to follow up to mentor him now that he was a new Christian.

"I feel so much better now that I called you," he went on. "I feel like a big weight has been lifted off my chest. I can die in peace now."

For a long moment as I digested his statement, the only sound was silence. Then he added solemnly, "A week ago I never would have dreamed I'd be having this conversation with you."

"A week ago I never would have dreamed I'd be leading you into a relationship with Jesus Christ."

"I can't think of a nicer person to have done it," he said.

For the first time during our conversation, tears filled my eyes. This entire experience was overwhelming. I'd been completely unaware that God would use me one day as his instrument to restore Uncle Norman to a relationship with him. Uncle Norman had been completely unaware that for the past five years I'd yearned to see him ripped from the devil's clutches and brought to the forgiveness in Christ that I had found.

Looking at my watch, I couldn't believe we'd talked for over two hours.

"I'm going to make myself a cup of tea now," Uncle Norman said.

"Okay. I'll call you next week."

CHAPTER THIRTY-SIX

On Assignment

Oh Lord, truly I am thy servant.

—Psalm 116:16(a)

I couldn't believe I'd told Uncle Norman I'd call him. My mind and voice had said the words, but it was as if the Holy Spirit had spoken them through my mouth.

I now know that God not only orchestrated Uncle Norman's phone call but also its timing. If he had called to apologize years earlier, I think I would have been too emotional to allow God to use me. As for Chrissy sending Uncle Norman a letter, that too was God's timing. She had done so in hopes he'd apologize to me before he died. But God had an even bigger plan neither of us could have imagined.

Wally was out of town on business, but I called to tell him what had happened. Then I called Chrissy and Sylvia. It was almost midnight by the time I managed to sit down for a bite to eat. The next day I ordered the large print Bible. The following week I called Uncle Norman but didn't get an answer. Sylvia called later to tell me he was in the VA hospital with pneumonia.

I called him right away. "What are you doing in the hospital? We have work to do!"

I spoke jokingly, but I was serious. While I hadn't yet mentioned it, I hoped to help him make amends with anyone else he may have wronged. I didn't have time for him to get sick.

"I was having a hard time breathing," he said.

"Would you like me to pray with you?"

"Of course."

I said a brief prayer, and he thanked me. I called every couple days after that, and our conversations always ended with prayer.

Since Chrissy was a victim of Uncle Norman, I wanted her to receive an apology also. I called her to see if she would speak with him.

"No, I don't need an apology," she told me firmly. "That wasn't the purpose of my letter."

"Okay, I just thought I'd ask."

Uncle Norman was sent back home, and my calls continued. In addition to our discussions about God and the Bible, he shared stories from his youth. He told me that when he was eleven and living at the orphanage, he'd stolen a nun's prayer book. When she discovered it in his room, she beat him. After that incident, he was sent to be fostered on a farm, where he was immediately put to work as a laborer. He ran away from the farm when he was seventeen.

As soon as he mentioned the farm, I remembered a story I'd heard from Chrissy years earlier. Uncle Murray had told her how

Uncle Norman was sexually abused while in foster care on a farm. For years I'd heard experts speak about child sexual abuse and read many books on the topic. I'd learned that many perpetrators of childhood sexual abuse were also victims themselves, though not every victim becomes an abuser. If Uncle Norman was a victim of child sexual abuse, it was no excuse for his behavior, but it did explain it.

Each time I called Uncle Norman, he shared different stories with me. During one of our conversations, I realized that God had given me compassion for him, something I'd thought impossible.

One time he spoke of his service in the army during the Korean War and how rats had crawled over him in his bunker on Heartbreak Ridge. For his service, he received the U.N. Service Medal, the National Defense Service Medal, and the Korean Service Medal with three bronze stars.

In our numerous conversations, I found him to be somewhat immature. I realized he'd been like that even when I was a child other than that horrible day he tried to murder me. I understood now why my mom had seen him as just an overgrown kid and younger brother when he was living with us.

During the weeks after Uncle Norman's initial phone call, he was in and out of the hospital several times for various reasons. Sometimes he was in for hours, sometimes for a few days. Because he was eighty years old and in bad health, I thought I should ask him about his funeral arrangements.

"Have you pre-arranged for your burial?" I asked.

"Not yet."

"Do you know what you would like?"

"I'd like to be buried in a military cemetery."

Since we'd had a military funeral service for my father a month earlier, I was familiar with the burial benefits for veterans. With Uncle Norman basically estranged from the rest of his family, I felt compelled to ensure he had a military service.

"Would you like me to make the arrangements for you?"

"Why sure!" he said with delight.

After many phone calls and letters, I found a local undertaker who agreed to accept the minimal amount Medicaid would pay for the basic services. I also secured a plot for Uncle Norman in a nearby military cemetery and pre-arranged a small military funeral. These were free benefits provided to him as a veteran. I also found a local Catholic priest to perform the service as Uncle Norman wanted.

Sylvia told me that Uncle Norman referred to me as his own Mother Teresa and that he'd told everyone at the hospital about me. He was amazed I'd pre-arranged his military funeral in accordance with his desires. He seemed genuinely happy about our relationship and always ended our conversations by saying, "God Bless You!"

"I feel like I've found a friend," he told me one day with emotion in his voice.

His words took me completely by surprise. I'd never expected to hear him refer to me as his friend. I looked at him as one of God's children who was in desperate need of help. The whole experience was very strange. I felt driven to help him as though there was a supernatural force at work in me. I believed I was on assignment from God and his chosen vessel for this most unusual task.

Mother Teresa was a Catholic nun best known for her work with the poor, the dying, and the lepers. Since Uncle Norman was estranged from most of his family, I wondered if he felt like an outcast or a leper and that was why he referred to me as Mother Teresa.

One day Sylvia called to tell me Uncle Norman was back in the hospital. When I spoke to him, he sounded unconcerned. "My doctor wants to transfer me to the VA Hospital in Boston for heart surgery."

"You let me know when it is," I responded, "and we'll pray together before your surgery."

We chatted for a while, then ended our conversation with the usual prayer. The next evening, Sylvia called again. "Your uncle had a heart attack late last night. He's in intensive care. The doctor said he's fading fast and doesn't expect him to survive more than a few hours."

"Thanks for letting me know."

The very next morning, Sylvia called again. "Your uncle passed away early this morning."

Hard though it would have been for me to believe before I became a Christian, I did not rejoice over Uncle Norman's death. This was a man who had misused the one life God had given him. But in the end he had shown remorse and turned to God for forgiveness.

The following week he had the military funeral service he wanted. Fewer than ten people attended, counting the priest. I was not one of them, nor did I have a desire to attend. I felt the assignment God had given me with Uncle Norman was complete.

Because Uncle Norman waited until he was eighty years old to commit his life to Jesus Christ, he didn't have much time to rewrite his epitaph or make things right with any others he may have hurt. But he made things right with God, and he made things right with me. I believe he went to heaven, and I'm okay with that now. I also believe I'll see him again someday, and it won't be awkward at all.

It's incredible how God used the most unlikely person on earth to help my uncle at the end of his life. Years before, I would gladly have put him in his grave, then spat on that grave. To be able to forgive and help him was a supernatural experience beyond my own strength or ability.

I never learned the exact reason why Uncle Norman tried to murder me. Nor did I ask him about it during the final six weeks of his life. My family and I still believe he became angry when asked to move out of our house and took that anger out on me. Whatever else might have taken place in his disturbed mind remains a mystery.

I still wonder why God spared my life when so many others who died young have not been spared, including my brother Ed. Did I survive because of Mom's prayers that night when she felt something was wrong? Or because I cried out to God for help when the first murder attempt started? Or simply because God had a plan for my life that was not yet complete? Or maybe all of those and more? I suppose I'll never know the answers to those questions until I get to heaven.

While I'm not perfect, to say that God dramatically transformed my life is an understatement. Perhaps a good analogy would be if I lost an arm in an accident as a child and God miraculously grew it back. That is how drastically my life has changed, both inside and out.

Without time travel, there was no way I could ever turn back the clock to undo the traumas I endured. But God has healed me emotionally from those traumas to the point that I feel normal. He has relieved me of the pain and hate I held deep inside towards my uncle. He brought that special someone into my life.

Some may ask why God didn't prevent my uncle from harming me in the first place. The reality is that God gives us all a free will to choose to do good or evil. Which includes me. As I look back, it's hard to believe my own appalling behavior during those six years before I became a Christian.

Although I did those things, it wasn't the real me. While it is no excuse, I believe my bad behavior was a direct result of the abuse I endured as a child. It was a long, dark period of my life when I seemed to have no control over what I was doing. I acted out because of the pain and tried to self-medicate in unhealthy ways.

Still, it was my free will that made those bad choices just as it was Uncle Norman's free will that made his choices. While I never physically hurt anyone, some of my actions were foolish and self-destructive. It was only God's mercy that I never hurt or killed anyone—or myself for that matter—when I drove home drunk. I have no doubt at least one angel was watching over me to guide my car safely home time after time. How else can I can explain how I arrived home unscathed?

After my uncle's death, I came to recognize more than I ever had before that the mercy God extended to Uncle Norman at the end of his life was the same mercy God had extended to me over and over. When he spared my life. When he asked a stranger to pray for me. When he sent my friend Jean to witness to me. When he healed me of my childhood traumas. When he gave me supernatural strength to forgive my uncle.

The six weeks God used me to help Uncle Norman before his death have demonstrated to me the depth of God's mercy. His forgiveness of my uncle is a prime example of Isaiah 55:7-9:

> Let the wicked forsake his way and the unrighteous man his thoughts; and let him return unto the Lord, and he will have mercy upon him; and to our God, for he will abundantly pardon. For as the heavens are higher than the earth, so are my ways higher than your ways, and my thoughts than your thoughts.

As I lay in bed that Christmas night so long ago wishing I was never born, I could never have dreamed the journey ahead would turn out as it did. At that moment I stood at a crossroads, not knowing which way to turn, which road might lead me out of the dark, frightening, storm-lashed valley where I'd lost myself.

I'm so glad I chose the road to mercy.

EPILOGUE

And Mary said: My soul doth magnify the Lord.

—Luke 1:46-47(a)

So what has happened in my life since I said a final goodbye to Uncle Norman? After Mom's funeral, I'd written Aunt Agnes to let her know of her sister's death. She didn't respond immediately, but around the time of Uncle Norman's death, I finally received a phone call from her. We made plans to meet, and I took the train to New York where Chrissy joined me in taking Aunt Agnes out to dinner.

Her personality was as crusty as the stories I'd heard, but God gave me great compassion for her. Over the next five years, we developed a good relationship. She prayed with me to accept Jesus Christ as her Savior just one month before passing away at the age of eighty-seven. So she is now reunited with her sister, my mom, and I have one more family member to look forward to seeing again when I get to heaven.

As for Wally and me, we will be celebrating our thirtieth anniversary in the spring of 2020. Only twenty more years to get that golden ticket! And for any who may be wondering, my friend Louise, who persuaded me to make that list and pray about my future mate, just celebrated her thirty-eighth anniversary.

Meanwhile, I retired from secretarial work and my jewelry business and have devoted the past few years to writing this book, being involved in my community and church, and taking care of our adorable Shih Tzu rescue dog. Wally is still a CPA, though semi-retired from audit work. He has been volunteering on our church's video team for over twenty years. He is still infected with the travel bug he acquired growing up in a military family who lived all over the world and still enjoys introducing me to new places and cultures.

Chrissy devotes most of her time to a foundation she started some years ago, using her analytical and oratorial skills along with her PhD in health education to help people inside and outside the United States. My former boss Patrick Enunzio and his wife along with Arthur and his wife Ann, whose prayers were so instrumental in leading me to Christ, have remained lifelong friends.

That my own efforts had not been able to effect any change in the laws dealing with sexual abuse crimes against children continued to weigh heavily on my heart. For years, I prayed that New York State would do something to address the statute of limitations (SOLs) on sexual abuse crimes against children. I saw a partial answer to my prayers in early 2019 when New York State passed the Child Victims Act.

While this bill did not abolish completely the SOLs, the age limit for victims of such crimes to come forward and press charges has now been extended to twenty-eight for felony criminal cases and fifty-five for civil cases. In addition, a one-year window (August 14, 2019-August 13, 2020) was established for any survivor of child sexual abuse to seek civil action even if their SOL has expired.

These new laws wouldn't have helped me had they been in place when I came forward in 1991. At thirty-six, I was beyond the age to press felony charges, and civil charges would have required Chrissy and I to pay out of pocket for legal expenses. Even if we'd been awarded damages, Uncle Norman was too penniless to ever have to pay them.

But if not perfect, the Child Victims Act is a step in the right direction and will hopefully help many survivors find justice. I continue to pray that one day there will be no SOLs in any state for criminal or civil charges of sexual abuse crimes against children.

I still count the years when February 13th approaches, and I thank God for each one. I also still carry in my purse the same laminated bookmark with the sculpted image of the little girl in the large hand, and imprinted with words from Isaiah 49:15-16:

> Can a woman forget her nursing child and not have compassion on the son of her womb? Surely they may

forget, yet I will not forget you. See, I have inscribed you
on the palms of My hands.

God continues to bring good out of what happened to me as I encourage others who feel hopeless. I hope and pray that in reading my story you too have been encouraged in some way. If God can help me, I know he can help anyone. If he can forgive Uncle Norman, he can forgive anyone who is truly repentant.

There was a time in the midst of my nightmare when I had come to believe that all I'd ever been taught about God was just a fairy tale. I am forever grateful that God extended his mercy to me and showed me again and again how very real he is. If there is one similarity to a fairy tale I can give thanks for, it is that God has indeed made my dreams come true beyond anything that terrified little girl could ever have imagined.

As he will do for you if you will but step out in faith upon his road to mercy. He's waiting with open arms.

ABOUT THE AUTHOR

Born in Upstate New York, Mary Therese Hutchinson is a graduate of the Katharine Gibbs School and worked for many years as an executive and legal secretary. Now retired, she still enjoys using her organizational and planning skills for community service. Mary's incredible story of secrets, survival, redemption, and transformation has been featured on The 700 Club. She lives on the East Coast with her husband Wally and their adopted rescue dog. Mary can be contacted at **www.marytheresehutchinson.com**.

Made in the USA
Lexington, KY
12 December 2019

58424926R10153